transbareall

TransBareAll:

ten years, still here

edited by

Michelle Green and Lee Gale

transbareall

Contents © the contributors, 2020.
Selection and foreword © the editors, 2020.
Cover art © Frank Duffy, 2020.

No part of this publication may be reproduced or copied, in print or in any other form, except for the purposes of review and/or criticism, without the publisher's prior written consent.

Published by
Bare Naked Books
an imprint of
Dog Horn Publishing
45 Monk Ings, Birstall, Batley WF17 9HU
United Kingdom
doghornpublishing.com

ISBN 978-1-907133-52-7
Cover artwork by
Frank Duffy

Typesetting by
Frank Duffy

UK sales and marketing: Inpress Books, 12 Mosley Street, Newcastle upon Tyne NE1 1DE
Telephone: 0191 230 8104 Email: orders@inpressbooks.co.uk

Overseas distribution: Printondemand-worldwide.com, 9 Culley Court, Orton Southgate, Peterborough PE2 6XD
Telephone: 01733 237867 Fax: 01733 234309
Email: info@printondemand-worldwide.com

The publisher gratefully acknowledges assistance from
Arts Council England.

transbareall

Contents

Note from the Editors — 13
A note on content — 17
Introduction to TBA — 18

WHERE WE'RE COMING FROM

An interview with the founders — Lee Gale and Jay McNeil — 22

Who, Where and When —
a visualisation of the first ten years of TBA — 36

SHOW & TELL AT TBA

On the importance of grandfathers — 41
Rob Clucas

embrace & expand — 48
Oliver Bonnell

The Transman — 50
Neil Bowman

I'm not scared to be seen — 51
Eilatan Hunter

10 Years of TBA — 53
Jochem

Silent Bonds — a photo essay — 56
Ludovic Foster

Gender-bound *Chris*	58

THE JOURNEY BEYOND

Moving into me. Transitioning to Judaism. *Jonathan Fernandez*	64
Fragile Men *Leslie Tate*	74
Fire resistant *Ludo Tolu*	75
Lost Souls *Joni Grace Indolent*	77
Re: ref/142HW88 – For your next appointment at the Gender Clinic, please prepare a one page autobiography focusing on gender *A Anon*	78
Breathe *Ben Hattingh*	83
Dear Torch Bearer *Caleb M*	84
Blossom *Jack James-Fagg*	88

transbareall

n.b./nb *Michelle Green*	89
A boy and his pussy *Leo Alexander*	90
Trans Punks Goin' Rural *Apu*	92
When he counts to ten *Tom of Tottenham*	94
Faded Green Door *BJ Christie*	97
Inside Out/Outside In *and* TransAction Man *Simon Croft*	104
Binary World *Alex Asher*	112
State Your Gender: Cisgender Apology *Rahil Cyril Virik*	114
Coping Mechanisms *and* Self Portrait *Anon*	117
Walking with Eva *Sebastian Buser*	118
Protocol *Little Frank*	124

Femme-city: How I came home to my Brown Womanhood *Beth Charley*	125
Gender drawings *Hidden Ink Child*	131
Saluting the Sun *Roadmap Zach*	137
Suggestions *Danielle Hopkins*	138
Un-male me *Ms Mocha Slessor-Parks (MichaelShe)*	139
Revolutionary Love *Nathan Gale*	140
Hearts and Nets *BJ Christie*	142
A bit on the side *Annabelle May Hampton*	152
Tree, Dreaming *Connor Rose*	153
Leaving Hibernation *Rahil Cyril Virik*	154
A FAB Trans *Lee Gale*	155

Cuddle Puddle *Max Alexander*	158
Tight Lipped *Remi Butler*	159
Conversations with No One *Benjen*	160
Cognisance *Logan Turner*	163
Moor Man *and* The Wilderness *Louis Bailey*	164
I Look Like A Farmer *Apu*	167
the female king and the masterpiece *MX Lupin*	168
A Continuum *Ollie Scharaschkin*	170
Non Binary *Serkan Kasapoğlu*	171
Invested *Crake Dakini*	174

bridesmaids wait [1] —
[they break their form below strange constellations,

half-formed twisting on their point of origin] 177
Beebee Vanunu

bridesmaids wait [2] —
[and what a country! white hills, an accumulation
of dust] 178
Beebee Vanunu

bridesmaids wait [3] —
[the dark's fire is an oil ground by gulphs of flame
that burst reclaimed in pitch] 179
Beebee Vanunu

Baggage claim 180
Harry Robin Hunkin

Dancing with(out) gender 183
Robin Hob

Transcape 190
Annabelle May Hampton

A Letter to a Loved One 191
Robin Prior

To Self…? 192
Léo Taylor

Cracked Ribs 193
Melody J Sproates

BLUEBELLS *Ben Hattingh*	202
on the High Street in the sunshine *Anonymous*	204
Life on Earth *Sez Thomasin*	205
The things I am asked are not really important *Frank Duffy*	209
Let the Children Boogie *Devon Bacso*	211
good timse bad splg *Beebee Vanunu*	213
Identity *Annabelle May Hampton*	214
Call me by my name *Ynda Jas*	215
#wewillnotbeerased *Harry Robin Hunkin*	217
Good Riddance: one Queer Jew's reaction to the toxic conflict between faith and queer identity *Sahaf Hardouf*	219

Rehearsal *and* Space *Franki Ayres*	223
Gender and 'I' *Sam Hill*	227
Kim *Allie Crewe*	236
The Strawman *Kira Nelson*	237
More *Lee Gale and Jacob S*	238
Floating World *Leslie Tate*	240
Death has no Language *Rami Yasir*	241
Build Queer Resistance *Apu*	249
Queerling Bodies *Daniel Morrison*	250
And through it all *Simon Williamson*	251

ENDNOTES

Glossary of Terms   254
Biographies   258
Acknowledgements   283
How to support us   287

transbareall

Frank Duffy

Note from the editors

Ten-year stretches: it's how we like to measure our time as humans, counting decades. In ten years a person can turn from a child to an adult, can build a life in a new country, can transition to the gender they have always been (and then for some a new one again). In ten years we have seen our climate change – our world gets hotter and less hospitable, and our politics more divided. We get more visible, those of us who live partially or fully at the edges.

And we find each other.

That's what visibility does, over time - it enables us to cross the distances between us and draw a map, mark a trail, swap details. This book exists as a celebration of ten years of mapmaking, of reaching out and finding others and actively creating space within which people with one sort of kinship can meet, connect, explore, and grow.

TransBareAll began with a desire to see just how tall we could stand without the weight of gendered social expectations on our shoulders. A space carved out of hostile territory, a window of time in which to feel free... and then another window, and another, and now, a decade on, TBA creates three or four residential events each year in the UK.

Ten years (as Lee says in the founder interview – 'ten trans years!') felt like something that needed to be marked. We tossed around a few different ideas about how we might do that, and as we talked we kept coming back to one present reality: every day we come across so many words written about trans people by those who don't know us and don't care to know us. The internet contains thousands of articles and comments and ministerial statements about us but without us, as the disability justice saying goes. We're being told more and more often that we don't exist, that we don't understand gender or sex and how it works, that we don't know our own minds and can't make decisions for ourselves about our own identities and bodies. We are mocked and doxxed and threatened and attacked in the name of 'family values', and those of us who are lesbian, gay, bi or queer know exactly where that line of reasoning has been lifted from. We have been here before.

Against this roar of patronising, pathologising noise, we decided that we would mark ten years of TBA by speaking for ourselves, on our own terms. A collective endeavour. We followed the path dug by the few trans writers who are now starting to get some recognition, and we took inspiration from the knowledge that within our community we have a huge wellspring of talent, knowledge and experience. We put out the call - and here it is, something quite extraordinary.

Within these pages you will find faith, and passion, and struggle. Anger. Laughter. Strategies for surviving a racist misogynist world, strategies for navigating parenthood. You will find sex (because this is not a children's book) and reckoning. Mountains and moorland, a cigarette scraped across the wall of a pub and a size 9 stiletto. You will find pieces of Lego that make sense of the world and a haircut at the best barbershop in London.

The words and images collected here were created by an array of artists, writers, and illustrators working at all levels of practice, from those newly driven by passion, to the seasoned professionals. It features work by cooks and educators, health workers and cleaners, scientists, programmers and students;

parents, carers, administrators and business owners, retail staff and civil servants. By people forced out of their vocations by disability, and by people working to change that. The contributors to this book represent a huge cross section of people who as well as being trans are every kind of person you can think of, because we are – every kind of person you can think of. For some this is their first publication, and for others this is one of many.

Within these pages are the love, the hurt, the humour, the power, and the bloody-mindedness that gets us through. This is a record and a defiant shout, a testament to the depth and breadth of our experiences as people and a community where we are the speakers, not the spoken about.

This is a collective work that exists only because of the labour, support, efforts and generosity of many people – please see the last sections for more information on our supporters and our glorious contributors! These ten years of TBA itself have been a collective work, made possible by the commitment and passion of many, but particularly all of our past and present management team members.

It has been such an immense pleasure and honour to work as editors on this book. This is the point at which words fail and body language takes over (and we are both criers!), so please just know this: we wish love and community to each of you reading this. And those of you who are part of the trans family, please keep speaking, and making, and being. You are tremendous.

– Lee Gale and Michelle Green

transbareall

A Note on Content
(and why we have not included content notes)

This is a book about people. About their lives, thoughts, feelings and experiences. These have been presented in a variety of creative ways, but always with honesty and openness. It is personal. It is emotional.

There are going to be things you will read in this book that may resonate with you, personally. And sometimes, these may be painful or difficult resonances.

As some of the pieces deal with particularly difficult topics, we discussed how we might best present those, including many conversations about whether to use content notes. We kept coming back to the fact that triggers - in the mental health sense of 'things that trigger a trauma response' rather than simply uncomfortable feelings - are both incredibly subjective and incredibly specific, making it almost impossible to provide a meaningful list of either trigger warnings or content notes that do not make assumptions about readers and in some cases simply reproduce the text in question.

So: please take care of yourself as you read, and take breaks as you need to. A book like this is a banquet rather than a snack - so take your time to avoid indigestion.

Finally, TBA is a body and sex positive organisation, and as long as there is enthusiastic consent we welcome work dealing with sex, nudity, BDSM, explicit language and so on. This is not a book designed for children.

transbareall

Introduction to TBA

TransBareAll started in 2009 with two at the helm – Lee Gale and Jay McNeil – and is now organised by a team of seven.

The idea was born from a project called the Transtastic Men Calendar, produced in 2008 to raise awareness of trans men and funds for UK trans organisations. The calendar showcased a variety of trans masculine models with differing bodies, and was a huge success, the biggest success being the confidence brought to the models involved, as well as a sense of community and shared experience.

Lee and Jay organised the first retreat in August of 2009, bringing twenty people together to explore on the theme of 'sex and body positivity'. TBA has continued to grow and thrive since then while remaining a trans and volunteer led organisation.

We now run three smaller, more intimate weekends of about twenty-five people each year, as well as a larger celebratory party event with up to sixty spaces. Each event takes place in a beautiful rural location over a weekend, focusing on a particular topic that's been suggested to us or by us. The smaller events provide a space for trans people to discuss and explore topics that impact on their lives, facilitated by the TBA team. The parties give participants a chance to run their own workshops on a variety of topics with support from the team. All events maintain a focus on emotional wellbeing, body and sex positivity, and a celebration of diversity within our community.

The trans community is forever growing and changing and TBA has tried to be at the forefront of that, working for as inclusive and diverse a space as possible while tackling themes and topics that people aren't always given the opportunity to approach elsewhere. Over the years we have dedicated retreats to topics such as disability, body image, consent, BDSM/Kink and non binary identities, for example, and we are always keeping an eye out for ideas and interest in future topics. Regardless of topic, our approach is focused on community and compassion, and, as Lee and Jay mention in their interview, on creating a space where people can feel free to challenge themselves in a supportive environment.

With TBA's ten year anniversary approaching, we decided in the summer of 2018 that we wanted to celebrate in style. We loved the idea of putting together a book of artwork, photos and writing from both participants of our events and beyond, and we decided to make it a reality. It has been a long, rewarding and often difficult process, but here we are at the other side.

The TBA team welcomes you to *TransBareAll* the book! We have been consistently amazed and in awe of the incredible submissions we have received for this book and we are so excited to share it with you. We are incredibly thankful to everyone who has submitted pieces, supported us and helped us work on this project. We could not have achieved this without our amazing community. We hope you enjoy it as much as we do.

The TBA team

transbareall

transbareall

Where we're coming from

transbareall

TBA Founder Interview

photography by Jake Herrett

Our editor Michelle spoke with Lee Gale and Jay McNeil, the founders of TransBareAll, to find out more about how it all started, and what it was that propelled us to where we are now.

Michelle: Tell me how TBA began.

Lee: We did a calendar called Transtastic Men where we photographed people in various stages of nudity. We started creating it in 2006 to sell in 2008, and it was based on the Calendar Girls film.

Jay: We both knew trans masculine people who, even though they had transitioned years ago and made changes that they wanted to make for their bodies, still weren't particularly happy with their bodies. And largely that was to do with not seeing other trans men, other people who'd made similar changes or who had similar bodies. I think a lot of trans masc people were looking at cisnormative ideas of what men should look like, and feeling that they were lacking in some way.

Lee: We wanted to make something that recognised that we can be sexy. We can have beautiful bodies. We can feel comfortable with our bodies, and go against the stereotype that if we're trans we have to hate our bodies and be depressed.

We sold nearly 400 calendars worldwide. We raised three grand. And we found that when people took their clothes off, the conversations changed. Because they had already bared their physical self, they were more open to baring other stuff as well.

Jay: People told us their self-esteem increased. Being visible and seeing other people with similar bodies, or very different bodies, made a real difference.

And not just seeing other bodies, but seeing your own through somebody else's eyes because of the photography.

Lee: Then we were at the Gendered Intelligence Trans Community Conference in 2008 – Jay was doing a workshop around mental health. I was doing one around sexual health and body positivity. We said, 'There's just no space to have these conversations where we're talking not just about if you put this body part in this body part, this is what's going to happen, but actually, asking, "How do I negotiate what I want? What do I want? What are my boundaries? How do I understand how to consent or say no?"'

We decided: let's do something. So we all met in Swiss Cottage in London, in a pub. There were eight of us. We started to have a conversation about what we could do. Then we hired a place in Chesterfield that could fit twenty people, thanks to my dad, who found us that place. And we got twenty trans guys together. On the Friday night I went to bed thinking, 'Oh, fuck. What have we done? This is the first time we've properly facilitated over a whole weekend.'

Jay: I was really surprised we could get twenty people who wanted to come.

Lee: I remember thinking, 'What are we doing? How are we going to make this happen?' A lot of responsibility came with that. Not only did people have expectations, but we had to hold people in that space. What we were asking them to do could be incredibly challenging.

Jay: We didn't start out fully formed, but we knew what we wanted it to look like.

Lee: I think bringing in the new team members really helped us, so that we weren't burning out and were also getting fresh viewpoints, and the flexibility to listen to what people needed from the space as well.

Michelle: *What kind of shifts have you noticed since then, in terms of trans and non-binary communities?*

Jay: I think that 'trans communities' is a vastly different concept now to what it was when we started. I mean, ten years doesn't feel like that long but I look back and, at the time, our context was national. What was the group that…?

Lee: FTM Network. And then Qwest.

Jay: There was the online forum, the Yahoo group. And FTM London, FTM UK – but we just wouldn't speak like that now. And then, you have *Boys Own* magazine. There was a real sense of masculinity in what you should be as a trans man that was projected through those outlets. That was our origin. As the community developed, we engaged more with different experiences and have tried to encourage that in what we do.

Lee: Neither of us have been the cisnormative male masculine, and neither of us have wanted to be that, but we saw those messages come from all sorts of different places and so with TBA we really wanted to create a space where people could just be themselves, rather than having to conform.

Jay: I was really early in my personal transition at that stage, and I felt pressure to conform to a certain idea, when instead I knew, 'No. That's not me. That's not what I aspire to.' We wanted to make TBA a space where people could be whoever the hell they wanted to be. It didn't matter what body someone had.

Lee: Or what body they wanted. What body they needed.

In the last decade we've seen a huge shift towards more fluidity around gender. We originally described the TBA retreats as being for trans men, and then as being for trans masculine people. Now we're having conversations about how actually masculine still falls within certain expectations of the binary, which is not always applicable for some members of our community. But it's really important we also don't lose sight of the fact that some of us feel very comfortable within the binary, within 'man'.

One of the things we found early on was that TBA became a really queer space. Which meant that those people that didn't have a queer experience or identity felt really marginalised and uncomfortable. Keeping all of those spaces for everyone is really hard, but we keep returning to the question: is everybody still feeling safe and okay in this space?

Jay: Having a wider team, people who have different experiences or different identities, helps us stay inclusive and keep developing.

Lee: Including cis people! The other thing that I've noticed is when we talked about accessibility; I think because we were open from the very beginning about wanting to accommodate access needs, people saw that, and went, 'Oh, okay, maybe I can do that.' Which means that when we have the annual party we have a disability caucus, and people are saying, 'It's really nice to have the space to be able to say, "Actually, these are my needs," and this is what's heard.'

And then also when it comes to diversity around ethnicity, one of the things with the trans community is that it's been, certainly in what I was accessing in mainstream trans spaces, incredibly white. We realised that that wasn't good enough, so we've tried over the years to change that, and be a safer space for people of colour and different ethnicities. That's something we're still working on.

Jay: I think that our whole conversation around accessibility has evolved. We have both learned a lot about what it means to create an inclusive space and a safer space. That's changed dramatically, which I think reflects the diversity we're seeing more of now, thankfully, in the community itself.

Lee: That diversity has always been there, but what we're seeing is more people able to say, 'Actually, I deserve to be part of this, and I want to be part of this, and you need to create space for me to be able to do that,' rather than people silently feeling, 'Well, I'll go to this event, but I know I'm going to be the only black person,' or, 'I know I'm going to be the only wheelchair user, and it's going to be crap because I'm going to have to get people to help me.'

Jay: Over the course of the last decade obviously TBA has changed a lot, but we have both changed a lot too. The creation of TBA coexisted with my transition, and initially I was feeling pressure to adhere to those norms of what masculinity should be. Creating a space where I didn't have to adhere to the norms allowed me to really ask, well, what is it that I want? Because I do quite like sex, and I like my body, and I like using my body in different ways, and that was not an okay thing to say ten years ago in a lot of trans men's spaces. We're meant to really hate our vaginas, and enjoy nothing from the waist down.

Being able to genuinely explore what I wanted and what I wanted my body to be meant that I made really good, informed decisions that I would not have made otherwise, and I might have felt more pressure to do other things. And my identity has shifted. I wouldn't identify myself as a man. Initially, for a very short period, I did, and now I wouldn't, because that notion is tied in with all these other constructs, and all these other values and meanings.

If I say I'm a man in our current context, it's loaded, and that's not who I am. And I love being trans. I love what that means for me, and through all that process, I would at the moment say I was more trans masculine, something like that. But I don't think it matters for me anymore, which is a nice place to come to.

Lee: I also appreciate having a space to explore what non-binary means to me, and whether that's a term that fits, and being able to see so many different presentations and understandings of non-binary, and say to myself, 'Do you know what? That word doesn't fit, but genderqueer does.' It made me go back to when I first started to transition and I found the word 'genderqueer', and I was like: that's me! But then I was shut down within the gender clinics. It says in my notes that was too confusing for them!

It has been liberating to actually say, 'Do you know what? I don't need them anymore.' Seeing people who look like men and are read by society as men saying, 'Actually, that's not who I am,' has enabled me to say, 'That's right.'

Another thing I've got is a real understanding of my boundaries. I realised I don't have to be the educator; there's stuff out there for people to access if they want to. That sounds bizarre coming from someone who delivers training on the subject, but I began to recognise that just because I do that professionally, I don't have to do that in my personal life. It's not my responsibility.

The other thing TBA has changed for me is understanding about my hearing, and that it does disable me. That I am disabled; I'm not just being lazy! And it's made me see what it's like to be in a space where there is an awareness of access. If somebody starts talking to me and then says, 'Oh sorry, I'm not facing you,' and corrects that, it means I don't have to do anything! It was such a big thing to negotiate that as well.

Michelle: *During the very first retreat, when did you get naked?*

Lee: We got naked the first night. It was in the evening after ground rules. At every residential event we set the space and do the naked etiquette. We ask the group: what do we want in this space, what helps people feel safe? I do remember thinking, 'Is anybody going to get naked? Or is it just going to be Jay and me prancing around naked?'

Over the years, people have come into this space saying, 'Oh, no. I'm not going to get naked.' And they've really surprised themselves by Friday night; they're prancing around with nothing on!

On the first retreat we needed to show other people that it's okay and the world won't fall apart. That first time was the only time I thought, 'Do you know what? We have to push ourselves or I have to push myself to show that this is part of it. Actually, it's a really valuable part.'

Michelle: *What's one of the standout moments, in terms of challenges with TBA, for each of you individually?*

Jay: There are two things that stand out as being moments which have been really difficult for me, but which I think I've developed from. I think one was — and I won't go into the situation — but I think the end result was a recognition that while we're creating and holding this space, at the same time we're still people and we still bring our own crap into the room. Having to be really mindful of that helps negotiate those boundaries.

I think that's been a learning point, on one occasion for me. It's the only thing I look back on and I think, 'I wish I'd done something differently.'

Lee: I think that's where, for me, having the team makes a difference. I mean, Jay and I were there for each other but we still had to hold a lot. Now, having six to eight of us on the team means you know you can share the load, which is joyous and beautiful.

Jay: I think probably the hardest thing for me has been where stuff we've done has come into conflict with some part of the trans community. You know, when we've done things because we've been asked to by some members of the community, because they want a space to explore X or Y. So we've offered those spaces, and then other people have been unhappy. We're not perfect but people are very quick to judge or criticise when you do something, without necessarily valuing that different people need different things.

Lee: I think because we do a lot of stuff that is challenging or taboo in other spaces, we can be quite easily open to undue criticism. It can be quite nasty and vile. In a lot of spaces it's a taboo to be naked, especially when it's not sexual nudity. We've done a couple of events and individual workshops around BDSM, and we have been subsequently accused of teaching vulnerable people how to beat each other up.

Jay: Yeah, we've had harassment. I think that's why I took a break and backed off. I just needed to retreat from it a little bit.

That was because of the actions of other people. It's really hard to manage that.

Lee: I think that one of the other things that's changed is that what we do feels less controversial now. We're seeing things we have done reflected in other spaces. When we started, we were the only space that did exactly what TBA does.

Jay: I think lots of people generally are told that bodies are inherently sexual.

Lee: I think that has been a misconception lots of people have had over the years: that if they come along they're going to be expected to have sex. Absolutely not. No, this is about bodies, exploration, and identities.

Michelle: *What do you do to take care of your emotional well-being throughout the years?*

Lee: We had quite a hard year in 2013. It was just… everything was horrendous. What came from that was actually realising we can't do this alone. People kept telling us, 'You need some help. You can't do this by yourself.' We were like, 'No, no. We got it. It's fine.' And then suddenly we realised, 'You know what, actually, I think they're right.'

Knowing that I've got the team around me helps. Knowing that I can send a message to our group and just go, 'Oh my God! Have you seen what's in the paper today?'

One of the things I've got from TBA is the huge connections, particularly with the people on the team, really close connections. But also with people that have been to TBA maybe just once. I've only ever met them once, and I've got a real, real connection.

Jay: I do lots of running. Running is probably one of the things I do to look after myself. I think one of the most important things is having a sense of community. I think that's absolutely essential for wellbeing nowadays. And realising that you don't have to do it all right now. Things don't have to be completely perfect. People are very forgiving, sometimes. We're never a finished product, and that's okay.

Michelle: *What is one of the happiest moments that you associate with TBA?*

Jay: One of my happiest moments is from the first retreat, of just standing there looking around and going, 'Shit, it's working. We've actually done this thing; oh my God.'

Lee: I think my happiest times are seeing when people open up, and they're trusting us, everyone in the space, and the space itself. And they feel able to share whatever vulnerable thing that is. After one retreat, somebody had talked about not being able to be naked at home, and then after the retreat they were able to go into a communal shower. You know, changes like that from just one weekend, a few days.

Jay: I think you're right. Just feeling astounded at what it's taken them to take those steps. The event that we've done that's held the most emotion, I think, would be the very small two-day workshop we did on loss. That was one of the most intense things I think I've ever delivered.

Michelle: *What do you see as the future of TBA?*

Lee: I want to see it continue to grow and learn, continue to happen, and to continue being challenging. One of our aims, as TBA, is to challenge. It doesn't have to be every time and it can be different things.

Jay: One of the things with TBA, when we originally set it up, is that it has to push some boundaries. The first five years felt incredibly edgy and then it started to be the same. We made a conscious choice then. We were like, 'How do we bring that rawness back to it?' We have to maintain that.

Michelle: *If you were to describe TBA in three words and three colours, what would they be?*

Lee: So three colours is an easy one. The first one is purple: the colour we chose for our branding, so it wasn't too gendered. Purple is the best colour ever. TBA is also a really bright, fiery red, because there are lots of raw emotions in it and that's how I view my relationship to trans as well. And the next one is green, because it's a calming space. I often arrive into the space going, 'Oh, I don't like my body. I'm ugly.' And I come out going, 'I'm fantastic, I'm amazing and I love my body!'

Jay: I think I would go green, because it feels like growth and renewal. And yellow, because it's sunny and bright. And for me – and you may disagree – glitter is a colour. It's definitely glittery. Everywhere. In all of the crevices, for many months afterwards.

Lee: My funniest moment: walking in with somebody having decorated their genitals with tinsel.

Jay: Oh yeah! It was vajazzling.

Lee: For me, the first word would be family. I think coming back to that theme of the community and connection. Then challenge, because it is a challenge to get us all there, to make it happen, to be in that space. And I don't know about a third one.

Jay: As soon as you say three words, I'm like, 'Naked bum fun. Vajazzled arse flash.'

Lee: You're all about the nudity.

Michelle: How do you manage to balance TBA with your other work and your wider life?

Lee: I work for Gendered Intelligence and I deliver training, so transness is my whole existence. And so I have had Carolin, my wife, telling me that maybe I should get a bit of balance and do things that aren't trans-related. I challenged myself by not being at TBA the last time, and that was partly to get that balance, to actually spend some time with Carolin, to connect with family, and realise I don't have to do it all.

TBA has got so much momentum and there are so many people involved in it that understand fundamentally what TBA is, and can create that space. It was an amazing moment to realise that it's its own thing now. And I think the other thing is recognising we can all be there for each other, and reach out and say, 'I need some help with something.'

Jay: Work-life balance is really interesting for me. In 2013 I didn't achieve it at all. We were delivering TBA, I had a lot of other stuff going on personally, there was the stuff happening in the wider world, and we were getting bombarded with harassment. The net result of that was having to walk away for a while. That's an act of self-care, but it has a toll. If you're trans, you're always working in a context of being trans in a hostile environment. And so having a space to be able to just go, 'That's out there. This is about me, and who I am, and what I want, here, right now,' is invaluable.

Lee: What's happening at the minute is that trans people are becoming more visible, and therefore more people are aware we exist, and therefore more people are confused or upset or angered by our existence. But it does mean that more and more trans people find out that other trans people exist. Although it's really hard for people, we can find each other, which is good.

transbareall

Who, Where and When - a visualisation of the first ten years of TBA

How old are the people who come to TBA?

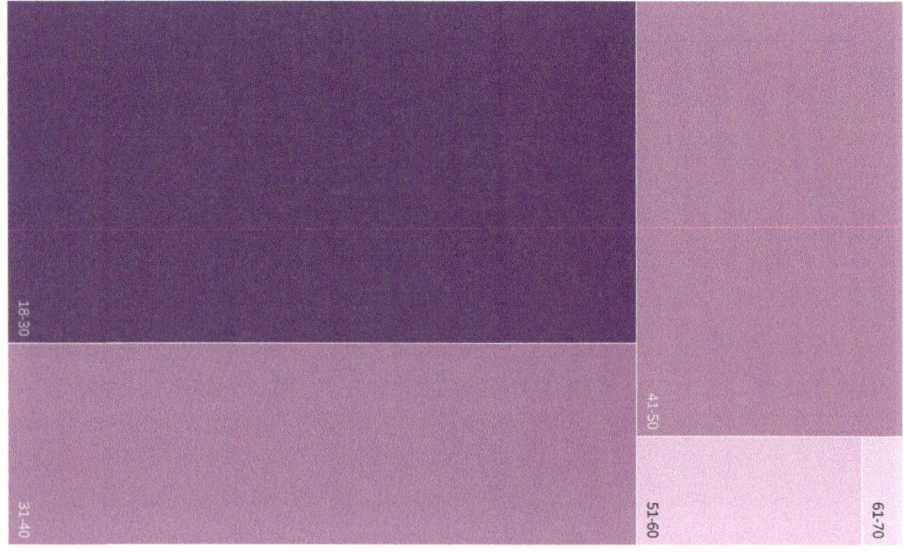

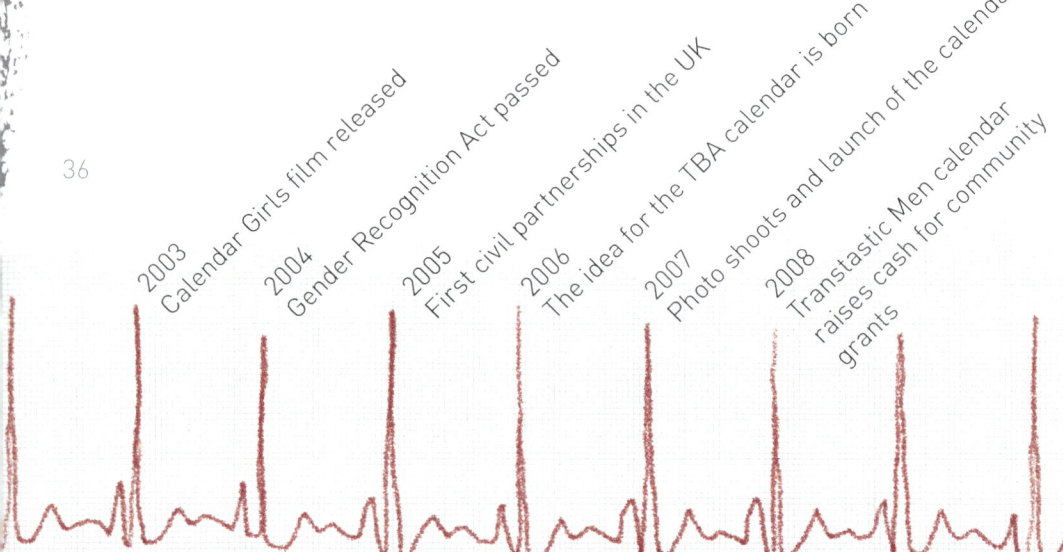

2003 Calendar Girls film released
2004 Gender Recognition Act passed
2005 First civil partnerships in the UK
2006 The idea for the TBA calendar is born
2007 Photo shoots and launch of the calendar
2008 Transtastic Men calendar raises cash for community grants

How often have people attended a TBA event? (one circle = one person)

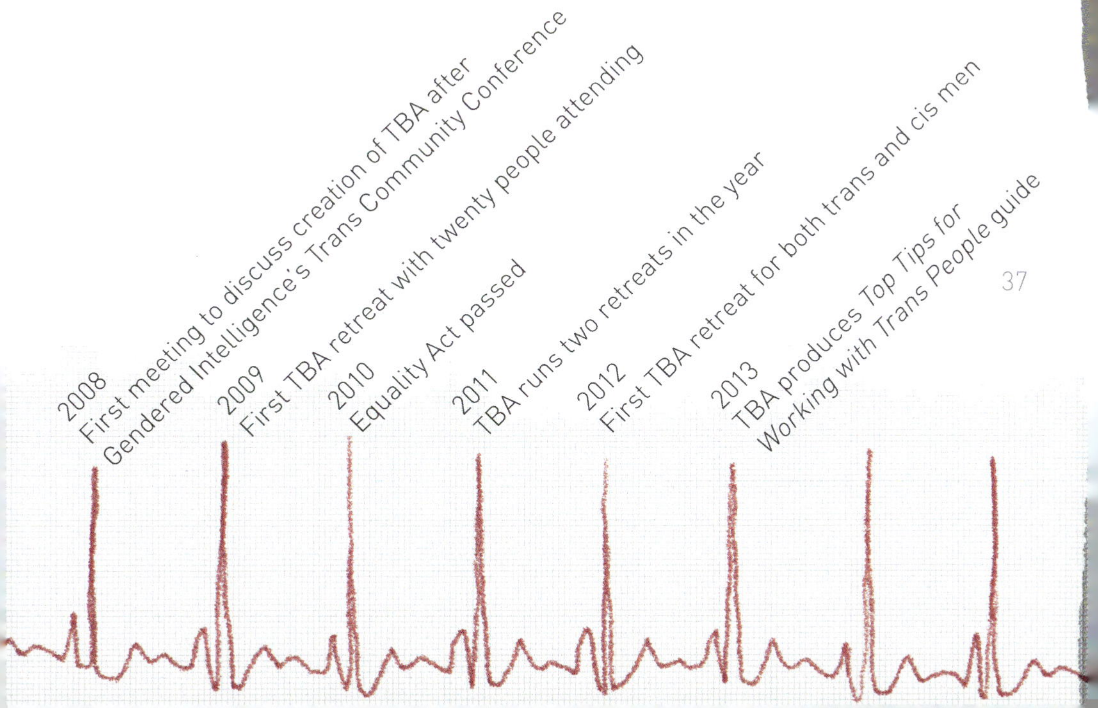

2008 First meeting to discuss creation of TBA after Gendered Intelligence's Trans Community Conference

2009 First TBA retreat with twenty people attending

2010 Equality Act passed

2011 TBA runs two retreats in the year

2012 First TBA retreat for both trans and cis men

2013 TBA produces *Top Tips for Working with Trans People* guide

transbareall

Where do TBA participants come from?

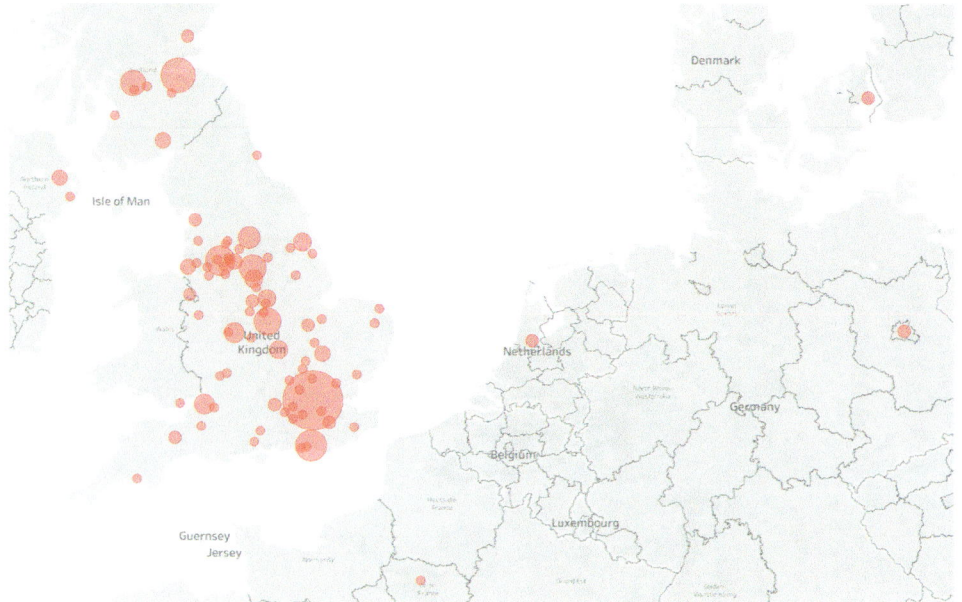

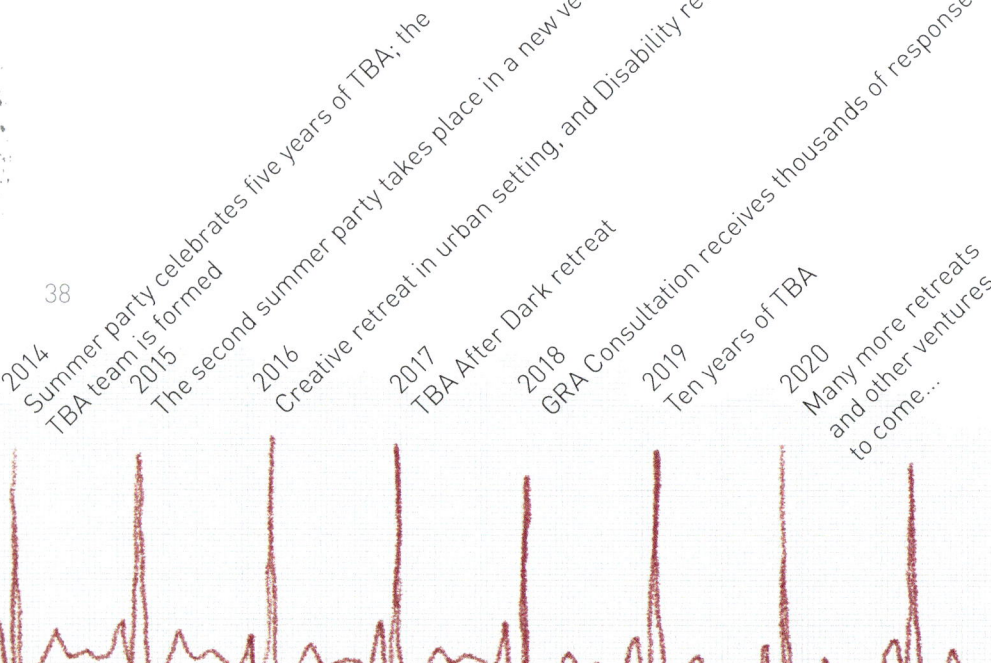

- 2014 — Summer party celebrates five years of TBA; the TBA team is formed
- 2015 — The second summer party takes place in a new venue
- 2016 — Creative retreat in urban setting, and Disability retreat
- 2017 — TBA After Dark retreat
- 2018 — GRA Consultation receives thousands of responses
- 2019 — Ten years of TBA
- 2020 — Many more retreats and other ventures to come...

Show & Tell at TBA

(spontaneous, of course)

transbareall

On the importance of grandfathers
by Rob Clucas

My journey with gender really began with my grandfather's death. It was a death that was both expected (he was old and ill) and shocking (he had been old and ill for many years — why now?). It was a death around which I felt guilt: I had prioritised a work obligation rather than visiting him immediately in hospital. It was a death that collapsed my world, as he was the one person I felt loved me without qualifications, without 'if only you were…' (thinner, more confiding, different). His death left me wailing, bawling on the impersonal linoleum floor of my parents' bathroom, stuffing a towel into my mouth to contain the noise, to avoid embarrassing and distressing the other people in the house.

I wept every day for six weeks and there was no comfort.

Around the same time as his death, my health worsened. It's complicated. I have a physical condition that was aggravated by me driving myself to do more, harder, faster, better, with increasing bodily restrictions, in a world that told me I should not have any pain, and it was all in my head. I worked myself to a standstill, to the point where I could not clean my teeth, use a knife and fork, or walk a few steps without severe pain. I endured, somehow, for a couple of years (because that was the main thing I knew how to do), until a change of GP brought me a proper diagnosis and a year off work.

A year off work! It was a year of pain and fear and uncertainty, but it gave me space.

One way I used this was an exploration of spirituality — a radical step, given my previously exclusive intellectual and physical focus. On that bathroom floor, I had bargained with God (who

I didn't believe in) to look after my grandfather's soul (the existence of which I doubted) if I went to church. Eventually, I went to church, and I found a home there for a while. There was a warmth and acceptance lacking from my work and family life, but also a sense of not fitting in that troubled me. I felt called to be elsewhere, somehow, and began to explore that. Was it a call to a different job/vocation? By the end of the year, I realised it was at least in part a call not to be married anymore. I was well enough to resume work.

My confidante moved away (another bereavement). I started therapy to try to untangle the mess of my life, as a lesbian (I assumed), married to a man I couldn't stay with, in love with a gay man who had left (you will notice the contradictions). I came out as gay, left my husband, endured the pain (because I know how to do that), and waited, waited, for the tumult to settle.

After about a year, I felt steadier. I looked God in their metaphorical eye and said, 'OK, I'm ready for what comes next.' But I wasn't.

Have you ever imagined you trapped the cat in the washing machine by mistake, seeing them tumbling over and over, unable to breathe, tangled in a mess of sleeves and socks and trousers, panicked by the wash, petrified by the spin? That was me. It was me from the moment I read Kate Bornstein's *Gender Outlaw* (I was teaching a new course on gender) and asked myself whether I was actually a woman, or...

I knew that trans *women* existed. As a young person, I'd danced with a couple at a women-only disco in York, and been driven by one of them to an early London Pride march. I'd written an (assigned-to-me) undergraduate essay on transsexuality (Caroline Cossey et al). But trans men? A theoretical possibility, sure, but I had never knowingly met one or heard of one except Stephen Whittle. How could I be one of these people that I could not conceive of? What did they look like? How did they sound? Were they outcasts? Would I lose my family and friends, my job, if I confessed how I felt? The questions, and the horror, tumbled me over and over. I hardly slept for a week; thought I was going insane; in the end I acquiesced, and the spin cycle finished.

Yes, I am not a woman, whatever a woman may be. Yes, I am a male person.

Jamison Green[1] writes of the discovery of his gender as lighting candles in a cave: each individual candle illuminates only a little of its surroundings, but when there is a critical mass, the cave's interior is revealed. This was my experience, too. Suddenly, I could pin-point the individual candles in my past: the conviction that 'girl's rules' didn't apply to me; the persistent sense of difference that I couldn't account for in other ways; telling my uncle when I was ten that I was not a girl, and tasting that statement's truth in its strangeness; the way that neither the label 'lesbian' or 'bisexual woman' fitted, despite some sense of match; the way I struggled with 'female' and worked out the rules so I would fit in and not be discovered; the way that being a wife felt so wrong; the reason I looked at myself in the mirror and despaired. Once I could see the cave, I realised that this was home in a way that nothing had ever been

---

1 *Becoming a Visible Man*

before, except my grandfather's love.

Realising my gender and acting on it so the world recognised it were two different things. To be at home in my gender was a process of public (very public) redefinition and boundary-making as I insisted 'I am male; I may not look it yet, but these are my name, pronouns and title.'

I did not lose my job. My most important relationships held firm, especially that with my daughter. Some friendships withered, and others were tested. I caused distress and embarrassment to my parents, and was estranged from them for some years, but we are closer now.

One of my most important sources of support during this time was TBA. I met Lee by chance at a training event, the day before my gender transition was announced at work. At last, I had met my first other trans man! I bribed him to talk to me with tea and cake.

Meeting Lee was pivotal for me; not only was he welcoming and generous, and a source of information about TBA, but he seemed to me to embody a comforting matter-of-fact queerness: an indubitably male person (no shouts of 'freak!!' on the street) whose life choices were not confined by society's stereotypes, or male typecasting. Here was a person I wanted to be like. TBA retreats, too, convincingly welcomed people – including me! – people who were variously warm, nervous, hopeful, reserved, outrageous, creative, withdrawn, overstretched, aspiring, centred, restless, relieved, naked, vulnerable, and diverse in various ways. TBA created and continues to create a space that is meaningfully and convincingly inclusive.

One special aspect of TBA's mission is body-positivity. In a world of airbrushed perfection, it can be difficult to feel male enough if one is not six foot and flawlessly muscled. If we add to this mix a female history, a variety of medical and surgical treatment, various body shapes, chests, genitals and scarring – you get the picture. But at TBA that does not matter. I am as real a man [or insert gender of choice] as I understand myself to be, irrespective of height, chest, genitals and how often I shave.

Being at home in one's gender and persuading the world to see you as such is a challenging process. Those who consider gender diversity as a delusion (despite our authenticity, and psychological/psychiatric verification) or a misunderstanding or perversion of God's creation (despite the vast amount of work we do on understanding ourselves and our place in creation) must be wilfully blinding themselves to the marvellous variety of ways of being people. Nonetheless, despite the evidence before us, society persists in its assumptions and stereotypes around gender. The years of social transition-without-physical-transformation were demanding, a perpetuity of yes-I-am-male-though-you-might-not-think-I-look-it-please-call-me-by-my-preferred-pronouns, of nervousness in public lavatories and changing rooms, of cultivating an everlasting 'this is me, fuck you if you don't like it' attitude. I must say that the Equality Act 2010 helped, because people in institutions and shops understood that they *ought* to be respecting gender diversity, even if they were not always good at doing so.

And now? Now, I am unhesitatingly read as male by anyone who meets me. I have a public history as a man. I have grey hairs in my beard. Although my transness is not a secret, and a quick Google search will reveal it to the curious, my gender history has become unremarkable amongst my colleagues and friends. New students no longer seem to be told my gender past before I meet them; old students forget that they knew it.

Passing as a cis man has its own challenges. One that I did not anticipate is the constraint of assumed conventionality. To be seen as trans, I need to out myself – and this is tiring, almost as tiring as defending my gender against those who did not believe it when they could not see it. But not to be known as trans – this is comfortable in everyday, impersonal interactions, but creates a barrier between me and those I might know better. In each repeated encounter with a new person, I gauge whether I wish to talk about myself, my family, my past, because to do so is usually to disclose my transness. If I do not uncover my history in some way, I remain at a distance from a new person, because I cannot be fully myself with them. But if I *do* make known aspects of my past, then I run the risk of being the tabloid trope TRANS MAN ROB, WHO REVEALS HIS SHOCKING TRANSSEXUAL PAST, or of being seen (wrongly) to extend an invitation to ask personal questions. The less energy I have to navigate life in general, the less willing I am to risk these encounters.

Some people would be satisfied with passing. Some people's goal is to be read as cis and never questioned. But for me, this is not enough. I have not left behind, excised or cut off the time I lived as a woman, and I do not expect to do so. My gender past is part of my present, even if that seems unintelligible to some people. I am male, and I used to live as a woman. I am male, but not a son to my parents: I am a male daughter. I am male, and I am a mother to *my* daughter. And, in the future, maybe someday I will be a grandfather.

transbareall

transbareall

embrace & expand
by Oliver Bonnell

My piece represents the sometimes turbulent relationship I have with my physical trans body existing in between the two binary genders. Society's influences are represented by the disruptive and disrupted sea and sky (in the cliché pink and blue). My body, as portrayed in the picture (somewhat generously) is reflecting and absorbing both of these expectations. However, as a result of the fantastic and profound impact of my experience at a TBA retreat, I stand tall and confident, striding between the turbulent forces, and held up by the confidence I gained by meeting other trans people who were happy and confident in their bodies. The piece overall shows the enduring effect on my self confidence that is the direct result of going to a TBA retreat — a space where I learned to love the skin I am in, despite the dissonance and alienation that broader society impresses upon myself.

transbareall

The Transman
by Neal Bowman

(Apologies to William Shakespeare)

Shall I compare thee to a cis-bloke
Thou art more lovely and more even tempered
(though that wouldst not be hard!)
Rough hands do shake my glue-on prosthetic cock
And my time with TBA hath all too short a date
Sometimes too hot the eye of dysphoria shines
And disclosure of my trans-ness becomes dimmed
At other times I feel confident and alive
No longer reticent to show my body untrimmed
But I am among friends at TBA
People who don't judge, who understand
All sexual identities; straight, queer and gay
Who can tell me what maketh a sexy man
So long as men can breathe or eyes can see
I am complete; a dickless man but whole on T.

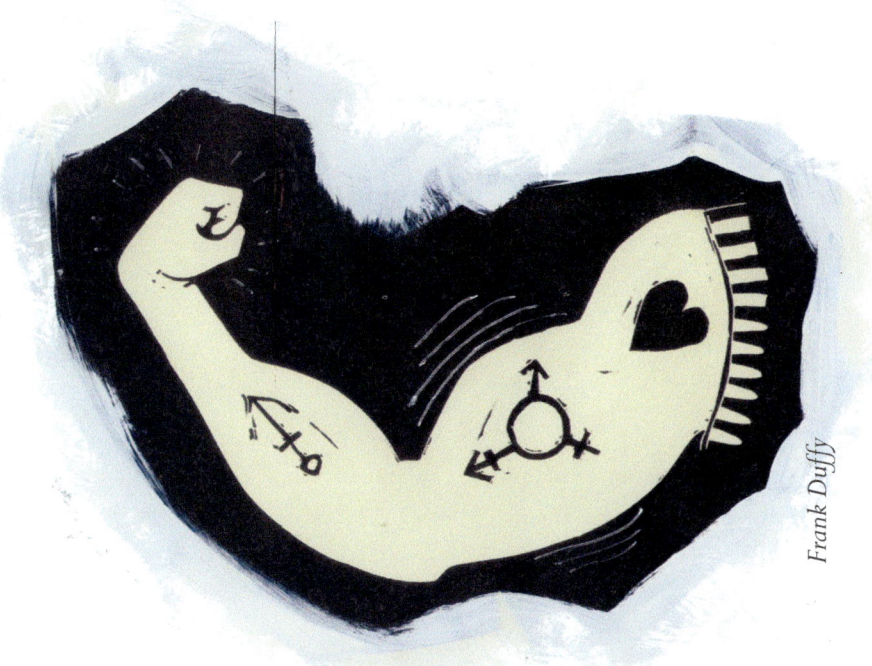

Frank Duffy

I'm not scared to be seen
by Eilatan Hunter

Gender as applied is something imposed by others without consent. I am a black pansexual trans man-ish.

When I first decided to medically transition, I wanted things to go slow. I didn't want testosterone at first as I thought changes would be too quick for people to accept – hell, for me to accept.

But accepting myself shouldn't feel heavy. Looking further within I realised it's the feeling of not being enough for someone, having broken parts that won't be fixed to perfection to fit with someone else.

Then again, what is perfection? It is what everyone should accept about you, not what should fit or what they think it should be.

Upon my discovery of TBA, I've realised I'm not alone in thinking or feeling like this. After this retreat and self-discovery I was able to express myself more so that the outward and inward selves match up, reflecting, mirroring one another.

Yet it's hard for outsiders to understand this concept. Maybe I'm still exuding some feminine energy, maybe I need to channel in more masculine energy?

Maybe I need to walk different, appear tough – anything to try to hide or rid myself of this energy I'm giving out.

But then, I thought to myself, my manhood is not determined by nor should it be dictated by society to be based on my outward appearance. Should I just fall in a box where it's easy on societal pressures to just tick a box and cast you aside to the rest of the gendered pile that there is and forget about you?

In a way, I feel sad being associated with male culture, because I don't understand it, it confuses me, and being socialised in that culture makes it even harder to relate.

I have stopped suppressing my female side and have now embraced, and by doing this I am becoming a better 'man' – in saying that, facial hair doesn't make one masculine, nor does the deepness of the voice or the width of the shoulders. What makes me a man is that I have embraced my vulnerability, my morals, self-conceptions, desires, the feminine/female qualities.

My body doesn't and won't determine my gender. My gender is one of power and one of disdain for power.

I am enjoying my journey into finding out what gender actually is to me!

10 Years of TBA
By Jochem

It was my first Transgender Europe (TGEU) Council, in Berlin in 2009, where I met Lee and Jay. They told me about this amazing project they'd done in 2008: this beautiful calendar with 'very decent' nudity. They showed me the calendar, and it was beautiful indeed. I was seriously impressed with the quality of the pictures, the compositions, etc.

Then they told me about this weekend for trans men, where they would be naked. I didn't know what to think about this. A weekend being naked?! Daring, no doubt about that, and also a bit weird, I thought. What would they do during this weekend, besides being naked? I had no clue. However, the idea would stick in the backwaters of my head.

In that time I was involved in the website Transman.nl that had evolved into the Dutch website for trans-related news, and information for trans men and their partners. In 2009 we organised the first weekend for trans men and partners in the Netherlands. It was a huge success.

So, when the announcement for the TBA event in 2010 came by, I passed it on to the Dutch trans men community. Meanwhile thinking that being naked (still) wasn't my cup of tea entirely.

In 2011 I met Jay and Lee at the next TGEU Council, in Malmö this time. And they told me about the success of the TBA Retreats, and they announced the third TBA. This time, I thought I should have a look at this mysterious weekend with naked trans men!

Together with my then-partner (and co-chair, as Transman.nl had turned into a proper Transman Foundation in 2010) I signed up. And boy, was I (positively) surprised! It was a very well organised, very good and very safe environment. As all other participants will know, we were invited to slightly move our boundaries, but not too much. It was a marvellous weekend, with lots of fun as well! Being naked turned out to be not that big a deal, after all.

After this weekend I thought it would be great if we could have a weekend like this in the Netherlands too. Due to all kinds of stuff it would take some years. However, in 2015 we were ready and started our own Trans & Bare Weekend (TBW)! Thanks to Lee and Jay we had a format, and we organised a couple of successful weekends.

It wasn't easy to find enough participants, as being naked seems to be a bigger deal in the Netherlands than it turns out to be in the UK. We Dutch people are very tolerant and accepting when we can say it, but acting on our words is something completely else.

I was quite surprised when we got requests for workshops based on the principle of TBW. So we also offered a couple of very successful workshops as well.

A highlight is the workshop at the 2016 TGEU Council in Bologna where TBA and TBW gave a workshop together. We gave an impression of our weekends. And we created a leaflet about the principles behind TBA/TBW, and a page containing some important tips for trans activists who like to create their own national 'naked weekend'. So many people were interested to join our workshop that we had to disappoint some of them, unfortunately. It was a wonderful workshop! Fun and good to do, and it was great to work with my colleagues at TBA.

In 2017 I was able to join another TBA Retreat. It was an excellent chance to see how much I had progressed in body confidence since my first TBA in 2011. In 2011 I wasn't able to do a full monty, but this time I had no problems with that. And TBA had progressed as well, being even more accessible than it already was in the early days.

A funny fact: this body confidence is not the only thing Lee and Jay taught me. In 2011 I saw them signing to each other. Although being fluent in Dutch Sign Language I couldn't understand a thing they signed. (British Sign Language and Dutch Sign Language are quite different, as are both spoken languages.) That annoyed me beyond what I can tell!

So, when I visited the UK again in 2014 to celebrate Trans Pride in Brighton with Lee, I made sure I knew the basics of BSL. That turned out to be a brilliant move, as the music was quite loud. So I could use my new knowledge right away!

(For those who might like to know: www.transenbloot.nl is the website of TBW. Here you'll also find the report of my experiences at TBA in 2011.)

transbareall

Silent Bonds – a photo essay
by Ludovic Foster

Negotiating Substance Free Social Spaces : Dining Room : Ludo

A place where people can begin to discuss what it might mean to have spaces and places within LGBTQI+ and queer circles to connect to one another without the aid of substances like alcohol or drugs. It can be easy for people in LGBTQI+ (and in this instance NB and trans, gender non conforming circles), to struggle with substance abuse issues to different degrees, because of the challenges that we face in a cis culture, and including other intersecting factors. The session will be a facilitated, substance free space for people to chat, connect and share as much or as little as possible.

SIGN UP : No - just turn up

FACILITATOR INFO : I am an independent academic, and community worker, originally from South Wales now living in East Sussex.

OTHER INFO : For trans and NB people who are in recovery, anyone struggling with sobriety in Queer LGBTQI social spaces and anyone interested in this conversation.

For me the experience of attending TBA was a personal test on many levels. I was intensely anxious about the train journey (because it was an unfamiliar route with quite a few changes), so almost didn't make it. And this was also a test for me staying in a social situation and maintaining my sobriety. I was proud of the fact that despite all these worries I came to TBA and even gave my workshop on trans addiction and sober spaces. Met some truly lovely people, and appreciated that it was a non-pressurised atmosphere where I could be myself and have plenty of quiet time. I also loved exploring a bit of the surrounding countryside, as these photos show.

Gender-bound
By Chris

In the 1990s there was a stark choice: transition or die. That was my personal situation. My bodily status quo was incompatible with continuing to live. To transition meant to live as fully as possible as the 'opposite sex', including undergoing medical treatments.

Unfortunately, the NHS gave ongoing encouragement for me to explain myself ever more, but gave nothing of substance in return. I was passively 'supported' for a year without information about social support and physical treatment options. Meanwhile, my dysphoria worsened and depression set in. The psychologist acknowledged that puberty blockers would do little for me, as puberty was complete. It was clear that I would be fobbed off for another few years, until one year after being referred to the adult services. I had no real choice but to seek treatment privately. I knew what I needed and, in my discharge letter from the NHS due to having a private consultation, my psychologist agreed: I would not change my mind. Accessing physical treatments was never going to be a quick process. The possibility felt so distant, yet gave me the tiniest sense of hope that I might one day have a physical form compatible with life. I was spurred on, too, by knowing that I couldn't kill myself and have my death recorded as female.

In parallel to any physical treatment processes, face to face contact with other transitioners, gender questioners and queers was essential. It provided fleeting respite from daily life, domestic transphobia, and a worthwhile return on the lunch money I saved to make the monthly trips from my rural home town. It was in a peer support group that I learned more about subversive and queer genders, though I don't think anyone described them to me in those words at the time.

At first, I felt such dysphoria that I wanted to have all available physical treatments. My naturally curious and contemplative nature served me well when I considered my gender and any treatments. However strongly I felt, I asked myself two questions before taking any step: 'can I continue to live like this?' and 'will this help me to go about my daily life?'

I was bloody relieved when the hormones stopped my menstruation, but the majority of wanted changes were at the expense of my voice. I am not musical or a performer, and I was not entirely comfortable with my voice. I stopped singing because of having to use the upper range of my voice. If I used the lower range I was taken as male on the phone which was fine. If it had been possible, I would have kept my voice as it was, while experiencing many other effects of testosterone.

The main distress related to the shape of my chest. I simply couldn't open up and stand up straight. This previous, closed posture is imprinted on my body to this day. Fortunately, I was able to arrange my chest surgery to take place in advance of going to university. This significantly eased the stress of daily life and being around other people, even though from this point on there were many mental and social adjustments to be made.

The more my body changed, the less I needed it to change. I actively and intentionally developed this. I recall a meditation session; I had never meditated before. Each person lay on the floor and at one point we were asked to notice 'the whole of your body'. Occurring at just the right time for me, I mentally connected with my vagina. I had had years of feeling detached from my body out of necessity for survival. I experienced this new connection as welcome and upliftingly emotional. I could not have anticipated it when entering the class. Until then, I was mentally detached from my body, as vinegar in oil. After the meditation, a few beads of mind-body integration were held in an emulsion, but the separation was a greater presence. This new experience encouraged me to continue to actively develop a stronger connection with my reproductive tract and strengthen my thought that, on balance, I would be better not having genital surgery.

Fast forward some years, and I met Jay and Lee in London.

Frank Duffy

During a conversation that day Jay said that they were thinking of getting together with a few friends and renting a cottage and just being naked together. Was I interested? I most certainly was! The following year, TransBareAll #1. 'Lumps, bumps, holes and poles' was the opening topic, if my memory serves me correctly. That fire was so delightful, and the show 'n' tell really was spontaneous.

At the national FTM get together after that I insisted that there should be a naked space. My persistence with the organisers led to having one hour in a crowded classroom with paper taped over the window on the door. People came and listened to the uplifting experience. Some people proceeded to bare some or all of themselves. I don't know whether anyone in that room later attended TransBareAll retreats, but plenty of people have in the last ten years.

As ever, contact with trans peers keeps me reflecting on gender in myself and society. I have seen the emergence and increasing representation of non-binary identities, including at TransBareAll. Surgical techniques and hormone options have developed too. I in no way regret the decisions I made in the past. They were necessary to enable me to keep on living. After very careful consideration, I made the best decisions I could at the time. As a non-binary person, however, I am often not visible. I sometimes feel that I am too transitioned to be (seen as) non-binary. As I have no desire to change my outward appearance, this tension is bound to persist.

transbareall

The Journey Beyond

Moving into Me. Transitioning to Judaism.
By Jonathan Fernandez

It's the question every convert dreads or expects. The question of 'why'. If it slips out at Friday night dinner with a new crowd, if it's mentioned in passing, if you've chosen to speak about your journey but carefully avoided *that* loaded question – for me, there's always that predictable moment of discomfort or frustration at having to answer the question 'why'.

I've come to expect others' inquisitiveness into my own life from being an openly trans person. People are curious and they want to know how you've come into being, regardless of whether it's a personal question or not. 'Why did you convert to Judaism, then?' 'When did you transition?' 'Was it difficult to become Jewish?' 'It must have been a struggle for you to come out at 15.' Conversion has, and continues to, mirror my life as a trans person in more ways than I expected it to when I first dipped my toe into the Jewish world.

So here's the answer to 'why'. I can't remember what I wrote for the Reform Beit Din in my personal statement. But looking back, now a year and a half on from when I emerged a newly minted Jew from the Sternberg Centre's mikvah, here's what comes to mind: trans people, like converts, are wanderers. Like the wider queer community, we roam from group to group, historical turning point to turning point, circles of friends, lovers, and teachers expanding and contracting like lungs. When I came out to myself as trans, I knew I was searching for something. I saw myself in two, five, ten, twenty years and I did not have a face, or a body, or a name – I couldn't fathom what or who I wanted to become.

If there's one thing I am afraid of, it is the unknown. I imagine my boggart would turn into a big question mark, hanging there in mid-air. As a trans teenager, inventing myself and slotting in the pieces of my identity to create some form of being, with a past, present and future, was the choice I made to stop myself from falling apart completely. There was no future for me as a woman; the way ahead was a haze of uncertainty, but there was one clear fact: I could not remain static and stagnant in a reality that felt wrong, dead-ended. In my imagination, in my soul, I knew who I was, and almost as if I was sent some miraculous knowledge from *hashamayim*, I eventually realised I could become something that made sense: a man.

Fast-forward through some painful surgeries, endless testosterone shots in the arse, a few cataclysmic low points, job changes, failed relationships, house moves and it's March 2016. Since I was 16, I was nominally pagan, but I had difficulty integrating any form of worship or religion into my life. I was spiritually lazy, unconnected and my thoughts about the Divine, about worship, about spirituality were grinding to a halt. Looking back now, I can't remember why Judaism struck me. It's probably a combination of factors, but it's clear that back then, I was in tune with something else higher than me. Beaten down mentally by a terrible living situation, trying in vain to catapult my religious practise forwards and find some sort of meaning in my career, I felt I needed something or someone to scoop me up, show me a sign, show me something that could help me fight my way out of this hole.

I *was* the 15 year old trans teenager, looking for meaning. I *am* a queer and trans man, searching inside himself for a spiritual path, a sense of belonging and understanding that ties in with my life as an outsider, as the odd one out, as someone different. I was looking for something combining the ritual and mysticism that

I'd grown up on as a pagan with something that I'd been missing, but not realised that I had needed in my religious life: a family.

So, like I did at 15, I jumped on my laptop, my feelings confused, not really knowing what the path that lay ahead of me would be like. All I knew was that something I needed was out there, and something inside of me had to change, was changing even as I read up on things that seemed so alien to me then. I remember opening 'Judaism for Dummies' and staring in awe at the words of the *Shema* in transliteration.

'I'll never be able to remember all of this,' I thought, as I lay in bed trying to recall those unfamiliarly textured words to my mind. Trying to make it mine. Trying to imagine it in my future.

It would take too long to describe my journey since that point. It feels like there's too much to make sense of, too much to wonder at. Joining *Am Yisrael*, like joining the worldwide network of trans people throughout space and time, has changed my life, and I can't even imagine where I would be without being Jewish — just like I can't imagine who or what I would be if I wasn't trans. However, the conversion process did feel remarkably similar to what I'd gone through a few years prior.

I knew when I became Jewish I wanted to be the best Jew I could be. Having a sudden panic about being behind in Hebrew class, I immediately practised Hebrew whenever I could, and I searched relentlessly on my own for answers to questions I had buzzing around my head. I brought this knowledge to class with me, and soon I knew that I had found something I wasn't too bad at: Judaism. Of course, this 'real life test' is something trans people know well. The rabbis who preside over your Beit Din – a panel of judgement when one finishes the conversion process (who are more welcoming and friendly than most doctors at your average Gender Clinic) – still need proof about the adoption of your 'real religion' into your life. What do you do in the Jewish community? What have you learned? Have you lived 'as a Jew' for a year and observed all of the holy days required? Then, and only then, with three golden signatures, can you finally call yourself Jewish. There is definitely a practical element to this. Being a social religion, learning the ins and outs of Jewish life is vital. Do you get the jokes, the current affairs, the chit chat? Can you walk and talk 'passably'? (Even though, like being a man or a woman, there is nothing a Jew is 'supposed' to sound or look like.)

Learning masculinity was probably more uncomfortable for me than learning to be Jewish. As a feminine, queer man, I didn't, and still don't, do well in 'men's spaces' – I am far more comfortable interacting with women and queer men, especially in positions of power. But Judaism from the offset was a place full of possibility and diversity, and I soon learned that in progressive streams of Judaism, trans Jews were welcomed and encouraged to live as their authentic selves. Learning about the different levels of observances, meeting Jews from so many backgrounds and who were all Jewish in their own unique way served as my 'real life' induction – that, even as a mixed race, Nigerian, Spanish, trans, queer person, I am still what a Jew should be – and that nothing is better or worse.

There are Jews who are secular and engaged in strong Jewish community activism, informed by passionate belief in *tikkun olam*. There are Jews who consider themselves culturally

Jewish — who like Jewish history, films, and food, but turn up to the synagogue once a year. There are religious Jews with a varying degree of practises and non-practises; there are so many different Jews that there must be (at least) one type of Judaism for every Jew in the world, just like there is no one way a woman presents her gender, or a man expresses his. Taking on the traditionally male trappings of Judaism was a powerful part of reclaiming my space and my body as a trans Jewish man. The first thing I did when I got out of the *mikvah* was to put on my tallit katan, a small garment with fringes, traditionally worn by men. After dressing, I replaced the kippah on my head — something I had approached wearing with trepidation, but now has become a fixture of my body, like part of my (receding) hair. A careful, wary stack of small cloth disks on my bedside, once viewed as something intangible, something loaded with meaning and power, have become haphazardly placed around my flat, or jammed into the pockets of coats for davening on the go. Living and expressing myself as a Jewish man moved from being occasionally sacred to becoming ingrained in my being, like a limb, just another fact.

Writing this shortly after Trans Day of Visibility, I am keenly aware that the power of being seen is something that religious people and trans people both have to navigate in various stages across our lives. Marking myself out as a Jew is something I do in the same way that I can't obviously mark myself out as trans - it's strange in so far that its relatively new; it's powerful, in that it affects profoundly how people treat me. Standing in line just off a 24 hour plane journey to New Zealand, there were two things that made the customs officer ask if I had any kosher food in my bag: my tzitzit and kippah, which, despite my dishevelled state, marked me out as 'other'. Less innocently, my rainbow kippah was what made a white non-Jew ask if I supported Trump at an anti-Trump rally. It's still difficult to get over the imposter syndrome, even though I've been involved in the Jewish community for a few years. I remember the terror when I first went to Kosher Kingdom in Golders Green – something strangely alluring, strangely nervewracking. It was like I was going out in male clothes pre-transition again, an invisible spotlight on me, even though I wasn't Jewish. I felt like I was playing pretend-Jew – and to some extent that feeling hasn't gone away in certain spaces: some Orthodox spaces which, as well as not seeing me as fully male, may not see me as Jewish at all.

For some Jews, coming into the fold and converting is like coming home into a people and pathway they always knew they belonged to. For others, like me, it's something that feels deeply right and makes sense, regardless of their prior background. Jews who convert, like trans people, have different narratives and different stories and different motivations for converting, or transitioning. There are rabbis who say that a convert has a 'Jewish soul' in them – that they have always been Jewish. Whether or not one thinks this speaks to us as converts, there is something that moves in the moment of conversion. Floating in the warm water below the primary school, I thought I could hear the creation of a world – distorted voices, machinery, silence, the rush of blood through the water of the mikvah. The moment where I emerged from the mikvah was one of deep shalom – a wholeness, and a rightness. Everything went in slow motion as I dressed, fumbling to tuck in the strings of my tzitzit to my trousers. And then the slap of cold air on my face as I emerged, born again, into the arms of the world. Discovering Judaism, discovering meaning, was something I had been looking for which accepted me – fully – as I am, and the sense of peace for me meant only one thing: it was the knowledge of the Divine Being standing over, beside and within me, joining me on the last stage of transition. I was read the words of Ruth to Naomi, a passage which all converts feel deep within their hearts: *For wherever you go, I will go, and wherever you live, I will live; your people will be my people, and your G-d will be my G-d*, and I felt something in my core reach back throughout time into the depths of my — now Jewish — spiritual ancestry.

In September 2019 it will be two years on from when I became a Jew, and eleven years since the very early stages of becoming Jonathan. I don't necessarily think I'm trans every day, it just *is* — even though I interact with my differently gendered body in the shower, or speak to trans friends every day. Just like I'm Jewish every day: I kiss my mezuzah coming back from work, I absentmindedly move my washing cup to clean a kitchen surface, I open my cupboard and am confronted with the unused plastic cutlery from last Pesach in the flat. Trans people are attacked in the mainstream media on almost on a daily basis and the encroaching wave of bigotry sends alarm bells ringing in my ears. A white supremacist kills Jews at prayer in Pittsburgh and Poway, and suddenly I can't breathe. I am Jewish and trans every day, as natural to me as opening my eyes in the morning and saying *modeh ani* — and I am Jewish and trans when my people are the victims of hate crimes.

The transition of the Israelite people in the Torah is something that still touches me, even above all the representations of gender diversity found in figures like Yosef and Rivkah, and other queer-ish Biblical figures. To me, the Exodus of these people and the journey in the desert speaks of a becoming, of a formation of an identity, an understanding of themselves. They set out of Egypt with trappings of idolatry clutching at them; they struggled with the fear that led to the sin of the golden calf, with what it meant to be a nation and what it meant to interact with others who had different lives to them; of what sacrifices and service meant, what following HaShem's guidance meant. They endured trials which made them stronger, they experienced euphoria at Sinai which made their hearts sing, which made them recognise their path and their future so vividly that they were terrified, but accepting. Becoming whole. Crossing over into the Land. Leaving things behind; taking new things with you. Learning who you are and how you have to live. All of this was my story, too.

What can I learn from the Torah's transition – from Breishit to V'Zot HaBerakhah? That everything in Torah had a transition of some sort: whether it's Moshe finding his voice and stepping into a leader's shoes, or Yaakov's change of name into Israel by a higher power. The transition of Adam and Chava from the bubble of Gan Eden to being cast outside their 'world', into a completely new, complex reality. From the indeterminately gendered Avram and Sarai becoming Abraham and Sarah, leaving behind everything they knew for a new life, to be true to their beliefs and their identity, listening to that inner call. Recognising bits of my own story and linking them to my transness is an act of reclaiming the Torah for me, making it relevant to my trans, queer narrative even with stories that aren't expressively trans or queer.

We are all created in the image of HaShem, *b'tselem elokim*. The first person on Earth wasn't a man, or a woman, it was a genderless, both-neither, being. The *Adam*, not a man called Adam. From the very beginning, trans people have been part of the fabric of Jewish life. From time immemorial, Judaism and Jewish peoples have transitioned, changed narrative, changed time and space and practise. This evolution is proud, and integral to what Judaism means to me. To evolve doesn't mean to eradicate what came before. It means to hold onto the past as a guide, to hold on dearly to the important essence of something but to step forward into a new era with new solutions and new challenges. Judaism is evolving, just like me. And that, I suppose, is why I converted.

Fragile Men
By Leslie Tate

The angle of his arm and thrown-out hand
is a bird of paradise flower where the sunbirds land.

She's in orange and black. In a blue-green softness
of love burning down, the hotness

and ache of blanched skin are he/she/they
seen through a glass darkly. If this is the way

of all flesh, root and flower of unnamed self,
then with what wings do we dance to our death?

Frank Duffy

Fire resistant
By Ludo Tolu

There are hard plastic cups and tequila. Sticky plastic cups. They bounce when they fall and when my foot hits the ground it sticks and I struggle to unstick it. Blow-dried hair flicks my face. I smell dry shampoo and I can taste the dirt stuck in the air. The air is cloud-like. It's a Blackpool night-club on New Year's Eve. It's sticky. That can't be right. It's heavy. It's a heavy, sticky air that seems to leave a residue on my skin. Or maybe that's my adrenaline-triggered sweat.

I'm keeping away from the inevitable bodies pushing and shoving and moving me away. All these unwashed hands circling. And my ears just want peace. There's no peace in night clubs. There's no peace tonight. I am alert. There are sounds everywhere. They should be cacophonous and yet when they combine they become noise that I'm filtering out.

I'm focused instead on the blank-stare of her alcohol-filled pupils. A blankness that brings no calm. I know to expect pain. I anticipate pain. Here comes an alcohol-filled breath shouting, screaming that if I were a man I would hold her like I owned her, like I possessed her.

Now is not the time to leave. I make sure she gets home safe. Then I suffer though more alcohol-fuelled tirades. But subconsciously I am planning my escape.

And three months later, here I am, escaping. The sofa is stuck. Stuck between two doors. Two white plastic doors, and I am jumping on it. This sofa is blocking me. I want to tear at it, and I want my tears to dissolve it or lubricate it out and into the front yard. At this point a film director would include rain as a necessary emotional touch. I could crawl under the sofa or climb over it. Or I could simply walk out the back door.

She used to mock my lack of strength. Saying I wasn't strong enough to be a man. But I know I don't need physical strength to push a sofa through a door where it doesn't fit.

Instead, I open the back door, pile the memories on ground mats and leave. And leave them to the rain.

Frank Duffy

Lost Souls

by Joni Grace Indolent

transbareall

Re: ref/142HW88

For your next appointment at the Gender Clinic, please prepare a one page autobiography focusing on gender.

By A Anon

When I was a child, I knew I was a boy. *When I was a child, I was child. I was a flesh and bone creature, barely human, feral and filthy in my habits, a wild thing of the common. I was cat and monkey and owl, I was soil and sky. I was a hundred people in a hundred books, far away and intensely here.* I played with cars and had no interest in dolls. *Witch-like, I collected bones and displayed them in a cave. I poked dead things with sticks and hid myself in bracken. I climbed trees with a book stuck in my pants. I was muddy, bizarre, sneaky, secret and chattering. Until I was ten and got glasses, I lived in world of shapes and colours with no edges. Nothing existed until it was a foot from my face, when I grabbed it and took it apart to see how it worked. I did the same with people, and still do.* I showed a preference for boy's clothes and never wore dresses. *Clothes were incidental to my existence, I put on what was there and never noticed what it was. I took my clothes off when the sun shone until I was shamed for it in school. A dress was never suggested, the idea would have been ludicrous. My parents didn't put straw hats on ponies or little wellies on piglets either.* I lived with my mother who was a teacher, and my father who worked from home as a translator. *See my privilege, doctor, I'm just like you. Tick the boxes, sign the referral. Shame rises in me like bile. I hate the hoops they hold for me. I hate myself for jumping through them. Until Mum qualified when I was a teenager, we played skipping games with the poverty line, the five of us kids, three parents in a falling down house, wearing clothes whose threadbare patches had known many skinny ungendered child bums and knees before ours. I was lucky, we were loved and had enough to eat, and I can yell at my kids in five languages.* I had one younger sister and my parents were married until I was 21. *Because only blood counts, doesn't it, they only want to hear about blood connections. Not the passing through ones, the loved and the loving, the connections by midnight feast and night time wandering, the others whose laps I slept in, who carried me and rolled me into a long bed full of bendy sleep-soft child limbs. Not the families of shared food and bath time and stories, of tribal siblinghood, alliances and betrayal, shifting family-things that slither out of the boxes and won't stay within the lines. Just one sister, then.* **I found puberty distressing and didn't like the changes that were happening to my body.** *I found puberty bizarre, incomprehensible, confusing. I felt as if I'd missed a chunk of school and nobody was telling me how to catch up, there was a secret rule book which everyone else had. Physically and socially, that was when I found that I wasn't ok as I was, so I watched people. I studied humans like an alien anthropologist, like a spy, and fabricated a mask so convincing that I thought it was my face for fifteen years.* **I moved away from home to go to University and spent some time travelling.** *Those were wild and messy years. I gave my body to be ridden by chemical deities who danced me like a marionette and threw me to my knees in supplication at the altar of forgotten things. There are cobwebby memories of waking like a defective detective, searching my body and surroundings for clues, of stumbling through days and howling at the moon, of sudden energy and spontaneous collapse.* **I married a cis man when I was 23.** *Nobody told me there were other options. Did I really not know, or was I afraid? I'll never know. She seems like a character in a book I read once, half remembered. I'd like to know her, but I think she wouldn't talk to me. She thought that everyone felt like her but didn't talk about it. I'd like to tell her that that's not how it is. She hid behind her mask and behind a hundred distractions, chemical, intellectual and biological.* **I had my first son in 2005 and my second in 2008.** *The perfect distraction, I didn't look inside myself for seven years. My eyes, attention and heart were outside my body, learning to walk, trailing clouds of glory. Years crammed brim full with wonder, graft, moments of desperation, sudden joys which burst like bubbles to fill my world.* **My marriage ended for reasons not related to my** gender or sexuality. *A decade of the dance between two people won't fit into words, and even if it would, the people who danced don't exist now. We fitted together, and then we grew and changed and didn't fit any more, even though we tried. We were flawed and complicated, we pulled out dark and ugly things from inside ourselves and threw them at each other, not looking to see their shape or the holes they left behind. Was it related to my gender or sexuality? I don't know, I'm not that person anymore and if I was, I wouldn't have the right eyes or the right thoughts or the right words to answer that question.* I became aware of gender diversity soon after that and immediately knew that I was not cisgender. *That first knowing felt like the first breath I had ever taken. The fear and the knowing burst out and filled me, all of me, the dark places I'd never looked, the dusty corners and secret rooms of me suddenly lit, exposed and open and the terror that came from knowing that it was never going away, this thing that had been woken, it was awake and alive and there was no taming it. Each small step I took, the new pants, the men's socks and shirts, turned off a warning light which had been lit in me so long I didn't know it was there. Every little thing felt like I was learning how it felt to be a person, to be real and alive, for the first time.* I have identified myself as a trans man for over four years now and have been taking hormones for eighteen months. *I haven't tamed it, but I've made peace with it. I've picked up many labels over the years and tried them on for size, tasted the shape of them in my mouth, and put them down. I mix identities like I mix metaphors, creating a conglomeration of sense and feeling visited sometimes by logic, and no one piece of it is the whole truth. Maybe I tell people what they want to hear, maybe I don't have a consistent sense of myself, maybe that's ok.* I have a strong support network within the queer community. *That's true, I've found my tribe and hold them close, but sometimes it feels like we're all at sea together. Sometimes we're playing with gender, splashing in the shallows in the sunshine. Sometimes I realise we've gone out too far, there's no bottom to the ocean and a storm* is coming. We're clinging together, held up by our linked arms and strength. There's pride and solidarity as we look at each other, but behind that there's something else, something that comes from the knowledge that we're not all going to make it, and every time I send a message or make a call, the words between the lines read, 'not you. Please, not you.' **I experience physical dysphoria and intend to fully transition.** *Genitals are always plural, but the pronoun of my cunt is a singular they. They – my plural, singular, both and neither genitals – are perfect as they are, and no disrespectful doctor with a not-knowing knife is going near them to normalise them for easy mass consumption. My chest remembers babies and lovers, pleasure and trauma held under the skin, which jars and scrapes. Testosterone has made them look as they are, nonbinary chesticles, furred like small soft creatures, so I can almost grudgingly forgive them for the terrible way they move. Almost. When the time comes for us to part company it will be with relief and gratitude. Like the pair of boots you can't throw away because you love them, but can't wear because they make you bleed, my gender and my body are both beautiful but don't fit together.* **I am comfortable and consistent in my male identity.** *Sometimes I think gender is like a Facebook quiz to find out what kind of biscuit you are, but the whole world forces me at every turn to choose between two fixed binary biscuit options, refusing to believe that the whole business is a meaningless stealer of time and personal details. My gender is like smoke, shifting and untameable. Put it in a box and it seeps out through the corners and cracks, showing the weak spots. I have no idea what gender I am, and I'm comfortable with that, and comfortable in my naked skin and soul. My demons live in the eyes of the world, the words and looks of other people. The Misses and the Ma'ams and the Mums shrink my skin and make my toenails squirm. Not from my kids, I gave the word Mum to them, placed it under their tongue when first they slithered, fishlike, from me. That word is theirs until they let go of it, given as a gift along with my blood in their veins. From the mouths of teachers, doctors, scout* *leaders it makes me curl like a hedgehog, hissing, shift from helpful engaged parent to fierce and fiery Other in a second. The Sirs and the Mates and the Misters settle in me, soft as feathers, stretching my wings and bringing me into myself. It's a box, and it doesn't fit me, but it's the only box I can stand in to exist in the world.*

Breathe
By Ben Hattingh

I'm tired of wishing I was dead, of drinking till I pass out instead
and regretting all the things I said last night…
'cause I don't want to frighten my friends, but pretending I'm
    fine is fruitless;
it's useless when I'm looking for outs everyday,
for ways to detach from reality.
Sadly, it took me a while to see that the change that I needed
had to come from me,
that being free isn't the quiet of my mind after my 12th drink
or after the next, when finding the exit sign is all that fills my
    head.
Instead, it's the safety of being accepted for me.
It's leaving home to find a new family
of friends,
of odds and ends:
a mess of people who respect you, who don't question you or
    your sanity;
new people who reinforce your validity.
It's clear to me that some people have a way of reminding you
how easy it can be
to just breathe.

transbareall

Dear Torch Bearer
By Caleb M

My dear, brave child, I remember your pain. You didn't feel different as a child, because you had no standard to compare yourself to which would make you question. When you started school, you had those first feelings of being different and just not quite fitting in. You were almost completely mute, responding only when it was necessary. The other kids had you marked out as different, as odd, and from that point on you were isolated. Banished from the realm of belonging somewhere. At morning break you would pace the playground alone, the loneliness seeping its way into your whole being. You never got upset, but rather resigned yourself to the fate that had been forced

Frank Duffy

upon you. Confusion set in, and at home with mum you would often question why you were so different. Why couldn't you talk? Why didn't you? At lunch, you would seek solace with the dinner ladies who supervised inside the school. You weren't really supposed to be in there, but they let you stand with them. It alleviated the loneliness a little, but not for very long. You left that school having never known friendship or companionship from your peers, and you hoped it would be different at the next school.

You started middle school with the rush of nerves that everyone has on the first day, however you had another reason to be nervous. You were depending on this fresh start to allow you to talk to your peers and make friends. The loneliness was just too much and you were so desperate to have friends. Maybe a little too desperate at times. One morning at morning break, you saw a girl standing alone and so you asked if you could stand and talk to her. She agreed, and by the end of the day you had finally made a friend. You came home and couldn't stop talking about it. It was around this time that you started to feel things you had never had before. You wanted to spend as much time with her as possible. It's only now that I'm older that I recognise what you felt was a crush. She was your first crush, and you did what any young and confused assigned-female child would do and suppressed it. You started drifting apart and made new friends because you were so afraid and confused by these new feelings. You went through a chain of friendships and, being so desperate to be liked, agreed to do some pretty silly things. You got in trouble at times with mum and dad for some of what you did. Going to see friends without letting them know. But you had friends, and for the most part you were able to maintain them - you had achieved that wish by the end of middle school.

Upper school presented a whole new set of challenges: the most difficult ones you had to face. This is where your bravery really emerged, as you always fought through it all. By now, any difference from the imposed norm was punished. And, well, you were pegged as different from the get go. But unlike lower school, where you were isolated, you were now a target. No matter how much you tried to hide, they zoned in and found you. The bullying was so bad in your first year that you lost three months' worth of school. You had to be gradually reintroduced to the mainstream as you just bolted out of fear when they tried to put you straight back in. Towards the end, you were met with tolerance from your peers. You never became friends but you left each other alone and they let you get on with things. You had other friends, and so this tolerance was actually a happy solution. But the damage from first year was done: you were left with low self-esteem, low self-confidence and self-worth. You were paranoid and untrusting. But don't worry – you get over that with some much-needed guidance, you really start to come out of your exile. When you left school age 17, you felt relief when you walked out of those gates for the last time. This began the next new chapter, and let me tell you it's the biggest one you'll ever make.

It's summer 2008 and at age 17 you're in a bad place, I know. It won't be easier any time soon but it will in the end – trust me, I'm speaking from that place.

Thank you for fighting for those seventeen years and giving me the resilience and fight that has been relied upon so many times now. At the age of 18 you hand over the torch and allow me to continue forwards and begin to really live. Nine years later, and the torch burns brighter than ever – and for as long as I'm alive, it will never go out.

With all of my love and gratitude,

Caleb

transbareall

Blossom

By Jack James-Fagg

n.b./nb
By Michelle Green

I carry a boy inside me, always have, feed him raisins and sealed bags of air, and this is not a metaphor about inner children and psychotherapeutic symbolism. The boy I carry inside me knows how to leap from the edge of the riverbank and crab-walk his hands across water-smooth stones, which used to be boulders, which used to be mountains, which used to be molten rock reaching for air. He knows that dresses are for people and makeup is for people and the sound of the wind moving the limbs of lodge pole pines is for every living thing. He knows which city side streets are shortcuts and which are really not. He knows that certain buildings cry out for soothing and he knows the weight of the unborn, and this is not a metaphor about miscarriage, or pregnancy, or all the things a body like mine is supposed to be able to do. The boy inside me eats raisins, sips from sealed bags of warm air, knows the weight of the unborn, knows that time is a hare stretching in the dark. He draws orange lines above each eye and watches the land rise to meet the rest of the known universe, and this boy is not a symbol, this body is not a poem, this poem is not a metaphor.

A boy and his pussy
By Leo Alexander

We're the ones your mother didn't tell you about,
the elephants in the room,
and except for TERFs and the occasional murder
the cameras won't ever zoom
in and the microphones won't be turned on.
They don't need to listen to ya, 'cause you're not a voting bloc,
not wealthy enough to throw money at political parties,
oppressed enough they can close our mouths before we're
    started.
Nothing but a number of bodies lined up against a wall
of hate and violence, and they're just waiting for us to fall.

And so, here I am,
a boy with a pussy,
I'm lucky to be alive,
40% of us try to commit suicide,
and sometimes it's really hard to want this life
of being misgendered and told I'm 'not right',
of being scared to use bathrooms so I get a UTI,
of having to bring up a dead name because having my data
    changed
is a privilege, not a right.

I'm a boy with a pussy,
so gay men don't want me;
straight men don't want me;
my family doesn't want me;
the government does want me, but mostly as a token minority.
Bisexuals are confused, occasionally –
asking, 'So how do you identify?' while we're doing it –
but at least I know the confused one isn't me.
And I'm sick of having to defend who I am –

that being trans is not a slight on the rights of women or anyone
    else,
that it's a constant fight for the right to exist,
that the burden is placed on these slight shoulders,
that the mere fact of being born enlists you as a soldier.

Two years:
that's how long Britain has to figure out what Brexit means,
that's how long it took me to first get my hands on hormones,
and while both of us think we're taking back control,
we're not, truth be told.
Because one day when I walk into A&E as a man
and they strip me down and find the unexpected, what then?
And when I'm forced to tell seven doctors I've never met before
that yes, I am who I am, so I can get my gender affirmed,
then I wonder - what more
do we have to suffer through?
How often do we have to conform to the cistem
or be left outside the door?

And so this is not just a story of a boy and his pussy,
wrestling with his family, his university, his peers and his past.
It's also of those who aren't remembered, who can't conform,
who don't want to conform, because gender's not about clothes
    or form,
and if a transgirl wants to be butch and I want to do drag
it's not for anyone else to dictate that this can't be the norm.
And therefore I implore
you – even if you're not one of us –
remember and fight for what's right,
so at least despite the fact it's a constant struggle,
we're not alone and we won't go gentle into that good night.

Trans Punks Goin' Rural
By Apu

When he counts to ten
By Tom of Tottenham

'One. Two. Three. Four.'
Stop. Count slower for me. Start again.

'One.. Two.. Three.. Four..'
Stop. I said slower. Start again.

'One... Two... Three ...'
Stop. You're making me cross. Slower. Start again.

'……..One'   The boi is bent over his bed.
My boi. It is late at night, quiet, a stillness in the air. His jeans and trainers an untidy mess on the floor beside him, his underwear pulled down and hanging around his thighs, his socks making it hard to stand still as his feet slide on the floorboards, his bare arse waiting in front of me. Perfect. Just how I want him.

'…….Two'   My leather-gloved hand gently strokes his arse. Even this softest of touches makes him flinch and tense, muscles straining. A sharp intake of breath. His fists grip the sheets, his knuckles whiten.

'…..Three'   He knows better than to rush his counting. He knows I like to wait. So connected in this moment so that nothing else matters.
He knows how this is turning me on, how hard I'm getting for him.

'……Four'   My boot lazily kicks his ankles further apart.

I hear him whimper as his feet slip, his legs spread, exposing him even more. I get a good view of what is mine, what I'm about to punish and fuck.

'……..Five'   He fears me more when I am silent.
No reassurance, no praise, no correction, just silence. He starts to cry. Tries to hide his face in the sheets. Hide his shame and fear and humiliation and wanting.

'………Six'   He hears me unbuckle my belt and slowly, slide it out of my jeans.
He knows this belt well. Let's see if he's lucky tonight. He's sobbing now, I watch him fight his need to tremble, his breathing erratic, desperate as he tries to brace against the bed.

'…..Seven'   I spit on his arse.
It is mine and I will do whatever I want to it. Now my hands are roughly grabbing at his flesh pulling and twisting and kneading. Forcing his butt cheeks apart to give me that view that I enjoy so much.

'…..Eight'   I step back to look at him, his body slackens as I take my hands away.
Of course we have played this game before. Of course I know what the anticipation is doing to him. Greedy little fucker. The boi who needs me to discipline him. To spank him so hard he'll be left with bruises he'll admire in the

morning. The boi who will moan and yell and cry but still remember to say 'thank you, Daddy'. The boi who wants me to see just how much he can take, how much I can have. The boi who I will fuck so hard that his tears and sobs spill into an orgasm, flooding his body with such force that he almost passes out. The boi who wants to make Daddy proud.

'……*Nine*' I raise my hand ready to smack his arse. Smack him so hard he'll scream in agony and relief. Soon he'll feel the pain of my leather-gloved hand striking his skin. Soon he'll feel what he craves yet fears. Because that's the game, that's what happens. When he counts to

'……*Ten.*'

Faded Green Door
By BJ Christie

At 37 years old I have finally worked out what's wrong with me. After nearly 456 months of puzzling over my life, the universe, and why I can't walk in heels, I have lifted the veil. It turns out that I am a 6ft chisel-jawed man with a goatee and huge biceps squished inside a stumpy woman.

Not content with plonking me on this earth in a body that's big on fat cells and short on inches, God goes and equips that body with the wrong set of genitals.

I now know why girl-clothes make me uncomfortable, and have a sensible explanation as to why I walk like a constipated Hobbit – but being able to label it doesn't make the pain go away.

I can pinpoint exactly when I realised who I was. It was during a television documentary called *Make Me a Man*. I sat and watched it at first with idle curiosity, then with tears rolling down my face, consumed with understanding and an insane envy towards that lucky new man.

My parents could never understand why I objected to wearing girly stuff, but back then I didn't either. They thought they'd adopted a little girl. That's what the paperwork said. Unfortunately, there'd been a mix-up at the factory and I was a grumpy Ken in a Barbie box.

As I trawl the internet, greedy for information, I am amazed how many people live lives similar to mine – puzzled and hidden lives. I found echoes from my childhood playing out across the world, and when I read of those brave enough to claim their hidden maleness, it both inspired and wounded me.

Only once as a child did I pluck up the courage to do that. It was 1974 in Weston-Super-Mare and I was ten years old, walking tall, as an hour before a shopkeeper had called me 'son'. I gathered my swagger and marched into the Gents' loos. The butterflies in my belly and the overwhelming sense of belonging still haunt me, as does the screaming row and punishment I suffered upon discovery. From then on, any glimpse of my forbidden masculinity has been riddled with guilt and disappointment.

But I still remember how, sitting in the cubicle, I breathed in the acrid smell of piss along with an amazing feeling of belonging and triumph. Several men came and went before my legs had stopped shaking enough to carry me outside. Those toilets are still there by the old pier but I don't know if the cubicles still have faded green doors. I haven't dared go back to look. Nowadays, I take comfort in locking myself away in my own bathroom with a knobbly old eyeliner, tracing out a homemade goatee. For a long time I was desperately ashamed of doing that – I still am to some extent, but at least now I know why I have to do it.

I bet Boots never imagined No. 7 being used like this.

My shame at secretive face painting is dwarfed by the terrible, twisted hope that I get breast cancer. Am I the only person in the world to feel disappointed that a mammogram came back negative? In my head, if I had the Big C, then I would have an excuse to get rid of the most obvious and upsetting feminine indicators. Reconstruction? Not a chance!

I feel terrible even allowing that thought to skitter across my mind on its twisted legs, but considering the Big Secret I'm keeping from everyone, I think that's just a footnote on the long list of things I can't mention at the dinner table.

I didn't think I would ever have the courage to tell anyone about the frightening mess in my head, until one unplanned afternoon I opened my mouth and spewed out my confession to a friend. I grabbed my alter-ego by the scruff of his neck on the way out and dumped him gasping and spluttering on the carpet between us.

She didn't bat an eyelid while I launched into the whole 'I'm not who you think I am' speech that might very well have signalled the end of our friendship. She just sat there and waited until I'd finished, then shrugged and said I was exactly who she thought I was. I might have had a gender-specific revelation, but I was still the same person she'd know for the past eighteen years.

Lesley is the only living person who knows the man I am forced to carry around inside me. Over Earl Grey and biscuits, I heaved up every excruciatingly personal detail I could think about him. I told her about how I strapped down my hateful breasts and about the fake dick I made to hide down my pants. I described how I put on a shirt and tie when I'm alone in the house, create my moustache and spend a short time feeling normal, doing things most people will tell you isn't.

I even told her I dream of performing sex as a man.

Like I said, she knows everything. She sat and listened while I described each intimate detail of that newly discovered man that lay on the floor between us, wet and trembling in the fresh air. She listened to his first confession as the layers of shame and ignorance were peeled away. My confusion that not everyone feels like a stranger in their own skin.

When I finally ran out of things to confess, Lesley laughed, and with a typical astute observation she said she now understood why we never clashed while shoe-shopping. Kitten-heels for her – work boots for me.

It feels rather nice to let the real me out into the open air in front of someone else, and although some of his secrets are a little bit grubby, I think he's beautiful. I haven't named him yet but I think it's only a matter of time before I do.

Actually if I'm honest, I'm a little bit afraid to put a name to him. It's hard enough to keep him hidden while he's still anonymous. If I give him a name, I'm scared it will be impossible to keep him locked away.

I am only now beginning to understand that I am different and if not totally freakish, then standing very close to it in clumpy shoes. I'm not however naïve enough to think I will get this calm acceptance from everyone. I have lived in this locale most of my life; I can't afford to move and I don't want to force my family to be cutting-edge in this little part of town. Life is hard enough for my children that I'm not the normal, skirt-wearing, home-baking kind of mummy. My mother tells me that I am selfish, that I need to grow up for my children's sake. She still thinks I'm rebelling to hurt her, when the only person that I'm hurting at the moment is myself.

It is so ironic that for years people have mistaken me for a lesbian

– even my own children have joked about it as I stomped around in jeans and boots, playing soldiers and building forts with them in the park. I took it as a by-product of my poor dress-sense and masculine deportment while secretly relishing the appellation 'butch'. I think it validated a part of me I barely recognised.

'She's a real tomboy,' they smiled when I was little. But what is cute at 8 is weird at 18 and downright creepy at 28, so I have tried to make other people more comfortable by squeezing myself into the pigeon-hole labelled 'wife and mother'.

Luckily for me my husband has never challenged my dislike of girl-clothes and feminine pursuits. He is happy to let me tinker with the carpentry tools and run around in a rugby shirt looking like I got dressed after losing a bet in a charity shop.

God, I love him – I really do, with all my heart. He is the love of my life, my soul mate and the person with whom I want to spend the rest of my life. The problem is, I don't imagine he'd want to spend his with another man.

Ironic to think that he already is, but doesn't know it.

Just prior to our marriage, I made a promise to his mother that I would never hurt her son. Unfortunately, I also promised my husband that I would never keep secrets from him. But here's the thing: if I keep the promise to him, I break the one to his mother.

I love my husband, I want to share this with him – I want to talk about this insane situation where I have a man living inside me. But how can I destroy his peace of mind by speaking mine?

This is the single most important discovery I have ever made. It defines who I am and how I think of myself, and explains so much of what makes me me, yet I can't share it with the single most important person in my life. What would it do to his self-image and sense of identity?

Unfortunately, I don't find myself the least bit attractive any longer. What little self-image I had nurtured over the years turned and ran screaming when it saw who I really was. It's one thing to be vaguely dissatisfied with your body – most people are, I think. It's quite another to be repulsed by something as fundamental as your own gender.

I wonder if this would be worse for a husband than finding his wife was a lesbian or having an affair? In some perverse twist another man has come between us – but that man is me.

I know I'd be deliriously happy to make love to him if we had matching genitalia, but I doubt very much if he'd feel the same way. I'm sure he'd be hurt and shocked to know I visualize doing just that, and I feel very guilty about being unable to help myself doing it. I'm just fantasising about myself, but I don't suppose that makes it any better from his point of view. I work hard at the gym so that my form has the muscle-definition I crave, if nothing else. It helps, a little. But not enough.

I have spent the first half of my life in a state of confusion and will probably spend the next half in disguise. Now that I know who I am, how can I face the years of deception?

I can't have the man I love and be the man I want to be. Self-awareness has unravelled my sense of identity and I'm busy scrabbling around at the loose bits, desperately pretending everything's fine.

I have to look forward to probably the next thirty years of hiding in someone else's skin. That's three decades of shaving my legs and not my face, 360 months of disgust at menstruation and menopause, mourning my absent cock. Almost another lifetime of pretending to be someone I'm not.

It scares me that the highlight of my masculine life could be the memory of the back of a faded green door.

Damn. If I wasn't such a tough guy, I'd cry.

Frank Duffy

Simon Croft

I'm a trans-man living and working in London. I transitioned in my early 30s, just over 20 years ago, and began making art at roughly the same time, partly to explore and express my own transition and partly to pursue a more creative approach to life generally.

My original inspiration was the photography and films of trans artists who document trans people and the diversity of the trans community. It was their work that enabled me to recognise my own trans self and I considered and still consider such imagery incredibly important, vital and validating.

However, back in 1998, it seemed that photos and film were all that there was, and at the same time as I was inspired and validated, I found myself uneasy. I was keenly aware that those photo-real images were easily read by an uninformed cis audience in reductive ways – do 'they' look like 'real' men and women? I knew we would be judged against norms, examined for traces of a history that would often be interpreted as invalidating our present and future.

I found myself asking, 'Where's the rest of our art?' Where was our sculpture, our object-making, our installation, our painting, our drawing, our collage, our stitching, our abstract work? Where was the work that could side-step some of those reductive readings and perhaps engage around gender more broadly, work that might arise from trans experience, but be understood more widely?

So when I started making my own art, and ever since, these are the questions I have been looking to answer; I've always sought different ways to discuss and explore trans-life, ways that resonate with trans folk, but also offer points of engagement to others.

I work with a range of materials that are not typical fine art materials – everything from beard hair, to flooring underlay, to slug tape, to drainpipes – an approach which reflects my sense of building my own body and self, valuing what is not often valued, drawing attention to things that are often taken for granted.

I believe creative works of all kinds play a vital role in broadening the visibility of trans people and in developing a visible and vibrant trans / gender diverse / queer community and culture. For me, a crucial part of this is about producing positive and celebratory works alongside works which look at some of the challenges we might face.

Title
Inside Out / Outside In

Materials
Wooden dolls, paint, mirror

Dimensions
Variable, depending on how the seven dolls are laid out, but fits in a space of approx 40cm square x approx. 30 cm high. Tallest doll is approx. 20cm high

About the work
'Inside Out / Outside In' considers the ways our identities are impacted by the approval or disapproval that the outside world projects onto us on the basis of our appearance, our behaviour, and our performance of gender.

Those of us who experience significant dissonance with these social demands around appearance and behaviour have to make choices regarding the extent to which we comply. And whatever those choices are, there's a cost attached.

For many trans people, the mirror is an extremely charged surface – it certainly has been for me. My reflection – in physical mirrors and in the 'social' mirror – was often unrecognisable to me – fragmented, incomplete and disturbing.

The Russian doll is a gender neutral figure – only when its surface is painted does it take on an identity. By covering these dolls with mirror – some fully, some partially – I seek to draw attention to that surface and how it functions.

Title
TransAction Man

Materials
Collaged photographs

Dimensions
Each image approx. 200 x 350 mm

About the Work
The twin images are based on a self-portrait, one incorporating parts of a 1970s Action Man – the kind I grew up with – and the other incorporating one of the latter models of Action Man from the 1990s.

Like Barbie, Action Man has been critiqued for presenting an increasingly exaggerated and stylised gender presentation as aspirational, and the discrepancies between my own fairly average, middle-aged, real body and the two toys are notable.

Whilst most of us experience pressures in relation to the ubiquitous imagery of certain types of bodies and associated 'standards' of masculinity / femininity, as a trans man, I sometimes feel this particularly acutely.

I am keenly aware that in our culture we are all brought up to think that we can reliably ascribe the gender of others based on their bodies. Further, we are taught that not only can we do this, but that we should do this.

It's therefore challenging for me to be naked in front of others. I fear that others may no longer see me as the gender I am if they perceive differences between my appearance and the cultural teachings of what someone of my gender should look like. I can feel very vulnerable because of this.

In addition, trans people still encounter intrusive curiosity and sometimes prurient or fetishistic interest in our physical form, especially around our genitals and concepts of 'The Surgery'.

In this piece I have used Action Man's pelvis to cover my own which both invites a degree of speculation and refuses an answer. It invites the viewer to consider whether they would regard me differently according to how the uncertainty might be resolved.

It also draws attention to the fact that Action Man is considered unequivocally male without typically male genitalia and therefore questions our cultural assumptions in that regard.

The title 'TransAction Man' suggests the idea that there is always a trade-off, a cost, whether we follow or reject extant norms and practices.

The piece can also be read in a multiplicity of other ways, for example as a comment on ageism, heterosexism, thinness, ableism or whiteness within aspirational 'beauty' imagery; or as queering the use of technology in our performance of gender.

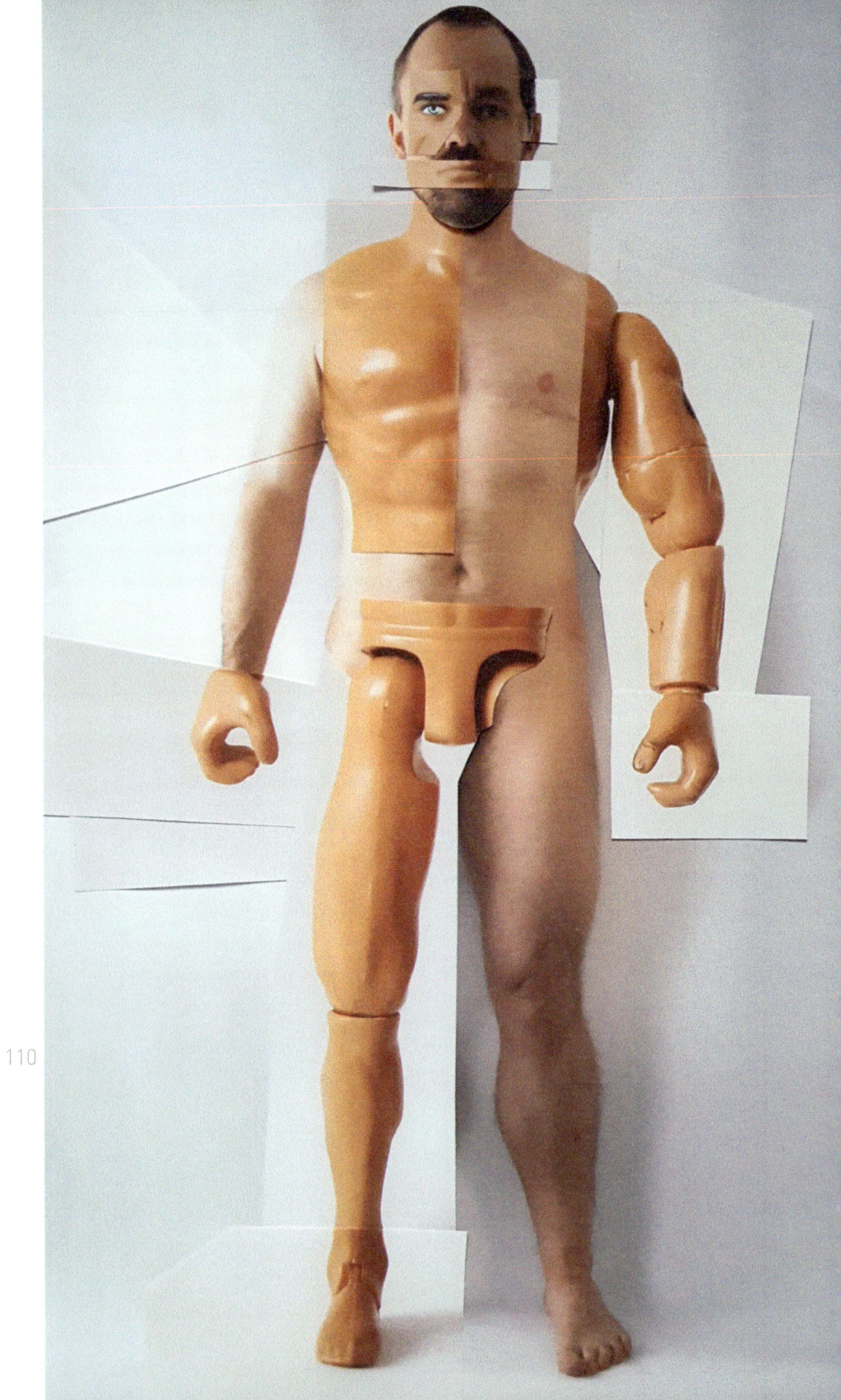

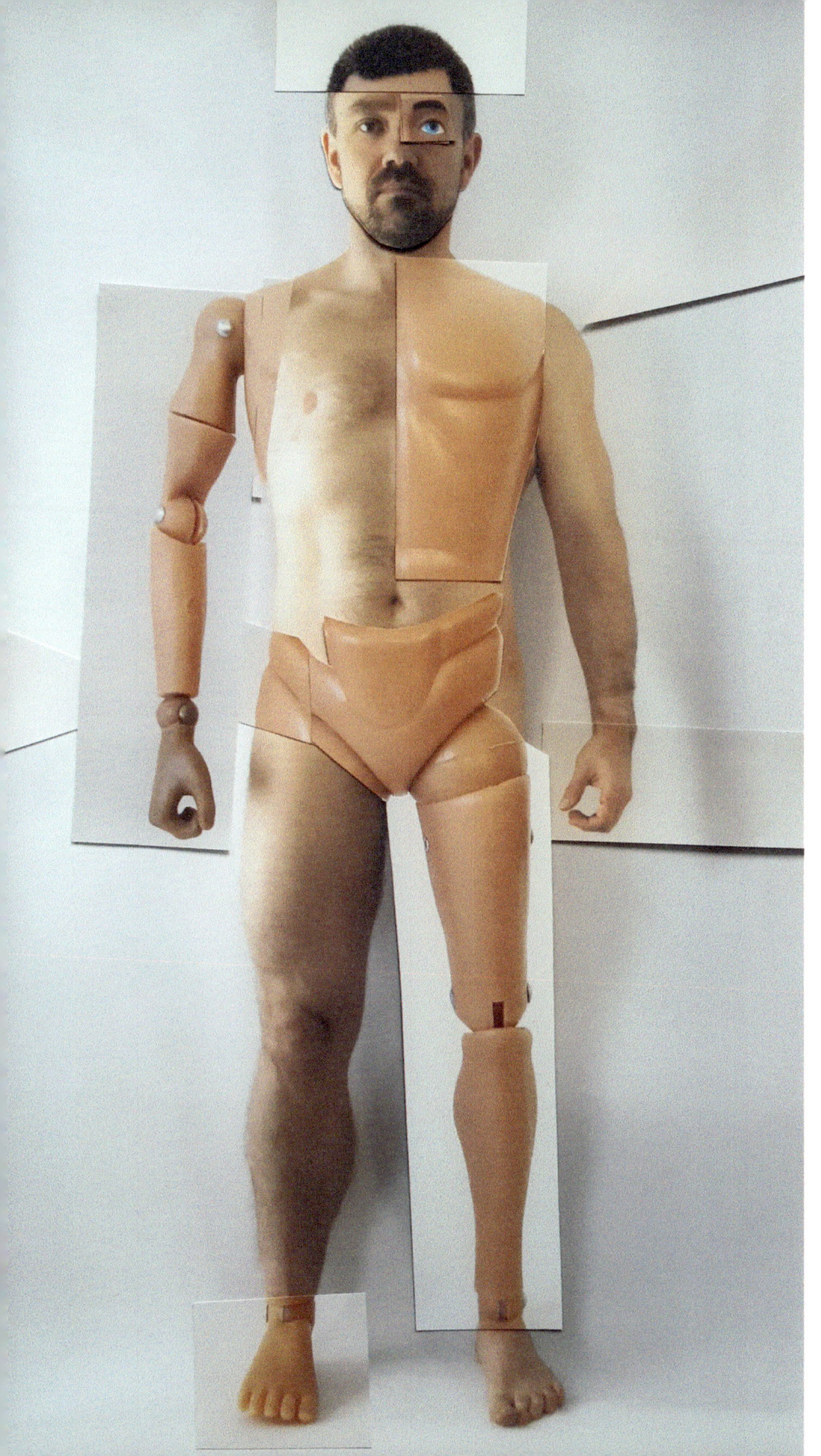

Binary World
By Alex Asher

Birthname Branded
Chest bandaged
Bound tight, tight, tight
A boy in transit

Things you all take for granted
become a daily struggle,
a hostile jungle
Is this hoodie baggy enough?
Does it make me look flat?
No blatant bumpy chest,
Will I be stared at?
Glares and abuse
from the men's changing room
Who knew it was so scary to pee?
In the queue for that one cubicle,
shoulders hunched forward
eyes cast downward
Don't want to be caught out,
For someone to notice
My hips too curvy
Chin too smooth
See me as some
Little Lost Girl, shouldn't be here.

But the pink dresses and eyeliner never suited me either

Yeah, I'm no masculine, macho man,
testosterone levels pumped up high
But no quaint lady figure neither.
Sorry to perpetuate stereotypes here,
I just want to demonstrate

how the rest of society seems to see the world
If you don't fit in one box, they'll cram you in another:
I can't be your sister so I guess I'll be your brother
I'm an ambiguous creature,
that's what school didn't teach ya,
People can exist outside the binary
Not just zeros and ones,
daughters and sons
The boundaries are just advisory.
Guess no one stopped to read the small print,
Notice our existence
Because I'm still stuck here
trying to camouflage my butterfly wings,
against the bathroom walls
Hoping no one will see
That I don't belong in the men's
or the women's
I'm just me.

Frank Duffy

State Your Gender: Cisgender Apology
By Rahil Cyril Virik

My gender exists, but they make me feel like it doesn't.

Man, He, Male, Bro, Lad, on and on they go projecting this masculinity onto me.

I did not fit into the feminine mould, so I sought the masculine mould instead,

and I blend in now. Many do not see the cut marks left from the scalpel, and those that do see praise me for how well I baked. Don't they see? It's just the icing on top.

My gender is not a secret, but it was concealed.

A game of hide and seek I played for years and years, never knowing what I was seeking, it appeared to me as a reflection in the mirror: the jigsaw puzzle that was my body, thousands and thousands of mismatched pieces all attached to resemble 'her'. I set upon reconstructing me, but with no box lid for reference, no picture of what 'me' looked like.

My gender is not unnatural, but all they see is abomination.

I wear their shackles of shame and guilt, sentenced by their ignorance and fear.

Always ready to shield them from the discomfort and bewilderment – the fault is all mine, after all, for how could I expect them to conceive beyond man and woman? It became second nature denying myself. The anticipation of their rejection held me back from pursuing friends, lovers, community, my pronoun, life itself.

My gender is not simple and neither is theirs.

I am living in this world, inhabiting it like an alien, part human/part obstruction.

They look at me with fascination as if I am some mutation gone wrong, morphed into a monster with just one word – Transgender. They call us difficult, thinking they are easy, but it's them I feel pity for, bound by these preconceived convictions of their gender, never glancing at their own reflection. You can't be transparent when you're under a cover.

My gender is not confusion, but they tell me it is.

They are so entitled with their thrashing, carving out these boxes as nature's law, ignoring the variations of the earth, where nothing comes in binaries when you look beyond your shadow. At first I too was mystified, but now I am unfettered by the unravelling of my spirit. Blessed are those who shine their flame; the journey is not clear, but we're on our way home.

My gender is not legal, but it is my truth.

My false identity is stamped into approval by the authorities, congratulating themselves for being progressive, while my kind and I gather the lists of our silent pain and compromises, ready to act out the begging we inherited. I tried so hard to be visible, for them to see the person in me, yet they are too entertained by my performance. To the cisgender, it's just a paper, but for me, it's

finally being written

into

Existence

My gender is not an apology

My gender is

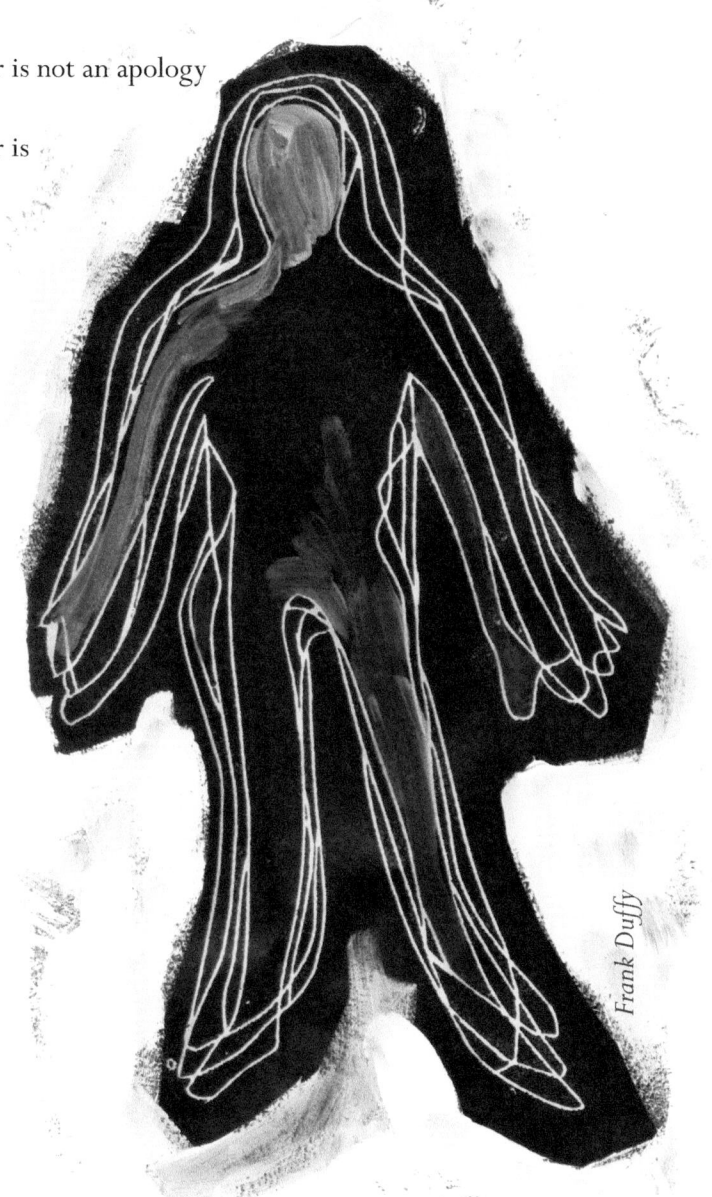

Frank Duffy

Coping Mechanisms *and* Self Portrait
by Anon

Walking with Eva
by Sebastian Buser

Adorned in a navy blue snapback baseball cap, I nervously set off on foot for a Haircut; my first hair cut as Sebastian, my first haircut with Open Barbers – a queer and trans friendly hair salon.

The walk is 3.2 miles from my house to Finsbury Park in London. It'll take me a bit a longer than usual as Eva Hayward[1] is joining me. We often stop to look at things; from the geometrical rhythms of the city facades, to the architectural weave of a spider's web and I want to ask her about what trans-becoming entails. By trans-becoming Eva means 'an emergence of a material, psychical, sensual and social self through corporeal, spatial, and temporal processes that trans-form the lived body'.[2] I am particularly interested in how my transitioning body may affect and be affected by my own familiar surroundings; what new sensuous delights are in store for me, I wonder.

Eva is from San Francisco, the Tenderloin district. She tells me that trans-becoming is a very personal experience, one that can't be universalised. She became interested in how her neighbourhood and her transitioning body interacted, in the sensuous transaction that took place; trans after all, she says, is a relational affair. We ponder the varying ways that transgender gets theorised, from the psychological, the sociological and even 'as some biological imperative'.[3] Although they have their merits these theories also feel unsatisfactory, like there is something they can't quite account for. Eva suggests that we might think about the 'expressiveness' of trans bodies.

---

1 This is an imaginary walk with Eva Hayward
2 Eva Hayward, *Spider Sex City,* 2010 p226
3 Ibid p226

She tells me that our bodies are 'creative reactions' and proposes a reading of the transitioning body as:

> 'a material force and… as an expression of bodily capacities, so I offer that the transitioning body is a reactivated, refreshed and resourced sensuous body, a phenomenological topography of affects and precepts that are changed in order to feel transposed corporeality'[4]

We walk silently for a while, I consider this idea of 'transpositions' as Eva calls it, my body as a porous entity, affecting and being affected by the streets, the buildings, people passing by – 'a continual motion of relations.'[5] Donna Haraway's words 'why should our bodies end at the skin?'[6] comes to mind. Unlike Eva I have not yet started medical transition but I feel the world is starting to respond in new ways I can't quite articulate. Nigel Thrift states 'emotions form a rich moral array through which and with which the world is thought and which can sense different things even though they cannot always be named.'[7] I wonder what new languages I may need to find in order to speak these yet unknown words. I have a fear that I will disappear, that transitioning will render me invisible, although I'm not quite sure yet what I even mean by that.

I tell Eva that I'm impatiently waiting for hormones and wonder how they will change me. I am also concerned how much I am

---

4 Hayward 2010, p226
5 Stewart, Kathleen, 2007, *Ordinary Affects* p2
6 Haraway, D. (1983) 'A Cyborg Manifesto' in Stryker, S. & Whittle, S. (2006) *The Transgender Studies Reader*. New York: Routledge. P103-118. p114
7 Thrift, Nigel.2008 *Non-Representational Theory* p176

co-opting into what trans activist/academic Paul Preciado calls the 'pharmaco-pornographic' industry,[8] the new economy of (techno)capitalism in which 'Technoscience has established its material authority by transforming the concepts of the psyche, libido, consciousness, femininity and masculinity, intersexuality and transexuality into [a] tangible [reality].'[9] Interestingly, one of the first uses of synthetic testosterone was self-administered by British trans man, Michael Dillon, in 1939. Preciado illegally self-administered testosterone as part of his research to be able to fully immerse himself in the processes and disciplinary regimes he was studying.[10] It was a political act he says, although now he too follows the protocol in order to keep up his regime of regular T shots.[11]

We discuss how I've often framed my life as one of learning, and wonder what pedagogical venture I want from this.[12] I recall Preciado stating that the body is a 'living political archive'[13] an

---

8 Preciado, P. (2013). *Testo Junkie: Sex, Drugs, and Biopolitics in the Pharmacopornographic Era*. New York: The Feminist Press at the City University of New York. p33. I also attended a talk where Preciado discussed hormones and the disciplining of sexual and reproductive bodies, particularly the pill. Preciado, P (2018) Talk: *Testo Junkie: Hormones, power, and resistance in the pharmacopornographic regime part of Transitional States: Hormones at the Crossroads of Art and Science* http://transitionalstates.com/ organised by Dr Chiara Beccalossi (University of Lincoln) with support from Wellcome Trust.

9 Ibid p34

10 Preciado (2013)

11 T stands for Testosterone.

12 This question is continuous and changeable.

entanglement of histories – from cities to design technology, to the invention of agriculture – 'your body is the body of the planet,'[14] he says. Testosterone then, is a form of amplifying the archive, a mode of learning about the processes of the body that are already present, chosen or not – a form of experiential learning. Testosterone may well be my new learning mess mate, my molecular travelling companion; a welcome addition to my already tentacular archival weave. However, I cannot yet predict what this entangled learning will entail.

Eva tells me that she often wonders whether the hormone treatment she started on – Premarin, which consists of conjugated estrogens purified from pregnant mare urine [15] – '[is] reshaping [her] species – becoming horse – along with [her] sex.' Eva asks: 'Could my interlacing mare chemistry be interlacing my own, giving me more insight into horse perception than sex perception?'[16] She says that her vision and haptic senses were noticeably altered. I too have heard the sense changes that testosterone can bring, particularly with taste qualities; people described either a loss of taste or a change in preference for bitter, sweet, sour or salty tastes.[17] Eva and I discuss how testosterone involves phytosterols, chemical compounds derived from plants – mostly soy, yams

---

13 Ricky Tucker, *Pharmacopornography: An Interview with Beatriz Preciado*, 2013 <www.theparisreview.org/blog/2013/12/04/> [accessed 22 December 2019]
14 Ibid
15 (which she does not advocate)
16 Hayward, *Spider Sex City* p242
17 These are from comments on a closed facebook group for trans-masculine people.

or sweet potato – as do new synthetic forms of HRT for transwomen.[18] Eva is working on a new text about becoming-soy for transwomen.[19] We laugh and I wonder what becoming vegetal has in store for me. Will it dictate what I choose to consume? How different will my becoming-soy be from Eva's soy? And how environmentally sound is the production of soy these days?

Pumped up full of soy-thoughts we arrive at the threshold of a hair salon called Chaps and Dames, in which Open Barbers have space at the back of the salon. As I see the sign 'Chaps & Dames' I can't help feeling there is an irony to this. I pass over the threshold. My pumping heart starts rising, emblazoned by imagined stares. I feel my trans-becoming amplifying. The witnessing mirrors outing this not-quite-there body of mine. But I must pass through here in order to get over there – the potential site of Urbachs anti-closet;[20] the space between closet and room – the site between Chaps and Dames and the street, the site in which fictions are activated and made real; a creative collaboration of my hairy trans-becoming, which I hope to carry through to the outside world.

I'm greeted with a smile. I'm offered to help myself to tea or coffee. There's a series of photographic portraits on the wall,

---

18 http://www.aaiclinics.com/how-is-testosterone-produced/
19 Hayward, *Spider Sex City* p247 note 3
20 Urbach, Henry (1996). 'Closets, Clothes, disClosure.' In *Gender Space Architecture: An Interdisciplinary Introduction* (2000), Jane Rendell, Barbara Penner and Iain Borden (eds), 342-352. New York: Routledge.
21 Angelus Squid Marr, *How dare you do your own thing with gender*, www.themolluscdimension.com, [accessed on 03/01/20]

some of whom I will come to meet at TBA. There's around ten zines pegged to a string line – I take one. It's called: 'How dare you do your own thing with gender' by Squid[21].

transbareall

Protocol

by Little Frank

Femme-city: How I came home to my Brown Womanhood
By Beth Charley

Hi, I'm Beth and I'm a failure at socially coded performative femme/female behaviour. No need to own this as 'self-confessed'. This was placed on me when they diagnosed me as autistic at 25, overthrowing the prior othering of the feminized lens of borderline personality disorder at 18. To me, BPD can be seen to be an entirely appropriate response to the trauma of living within the binarised artificial straitjacket of capitalistic action and reaction, dependence and interdependence that is shaped by a paternalistic whiteness; where 'curious' behaviour is often coded as a sign of illness, or even malignancy. Whereas autism is seen as a deviation from an active norm that codes male-socialised people through an even narrower lens of them losing access to their depth of emotion, and their female counterparts get consumed by the burden of that caretaking.

Keeping up with me so far? Are you sitting comfortably? Then let us begin our anthropological study into 'white' ,'normal', 'preference' driven society and how they treat their animals... no their children... no their 'others'... the 'people' who colour outside the margins of the written instructions inherent in prolonging the factory conditions without union representation. To meet the endless externalised worth-y seeking consumer demand for misguided solace and personal equity. But know this...there is no room for tapestry in rainbows or even beyond the binary hue placed on them at birth.

In the wise words of the great Todrick Hall: 'Reach, but not too wide / Think the impossible as long as it's in black and white'.

In fact that song, 'Black and White', provides the perfect social backdrop to talk about difference and those of us who choose to live in the margins because we feel safer in the shadows or have been told we inhabit no mans' land because of the gap between our socially coded and perceived container and how we drive our vehicle. Or those of us who flit between the two states of being and doing and then end up in the exhaustion of constantly being told we need to pick a side without access to the instructions that will keep us well in that camp.

I could carry on about how the gender binary is more an internalised/traumatised social experience, a simultaneously symbiotic unconscious running the script of a power structure that hides in plain sight; and how we need embodied narratives about the impact of our socialised childhoods that so affect our behaviour and how we treat each other, but you can read that in a book I hopefully intend to write once I have devised a more compassionate term than 'critical thinking' or 'emotional literacy', because even those don't have the depth of currency and absence of kindness resonant with how we treat our young so insidiously. I was invited to contribute for who I am and how I see the world. Overt feminist aiming for intersectional positionality and embodied knowledge for the win.

And so to undo some of the censoring and silencing from a world that sees me as too much and intimidating; from an ex who told me I only talk about myself in debates about structural power threads, to my most recent who could not see me and the care I needed in weaving instances of his behaviour that contributed to me feeling unsafe and almost coerced into taking responsibility for his feelings. The latter is a common occurrence under the patriarchal eye, but like the glamourous Ariana says 'I've loved and I've lost / But that's not what I see / So, look what I got / Look what you taught me' And as the glorious poet Nayyirah Waheed concludes: 'if you are *softer* than before they came; you have been loved' (emphasis and punctuation my own).

So, let me introduce myself... just what hand of cards has this life dealt me? What have I got? Who am I? Typically, I find myself often characterised in absence; but not silent witness. Recently, I was asked to take part in a disability panel. I was anxious for two main reasons, well three, being my first solo polyamory event after a decade in my own echo chamber – but there is work pending on that front under the banner of my journey 'in search of soulidarity'. What created butterflies in my stomach (not the good kind), was that it was the first time I had overtly claimed my card as a disabled by society person and additionally was my first speaking engagement outside of the autismsphere.

I was the only English, English-speaker in the room – this event taking place in sunny San Francisco and I was one of four people of female-socialised perspectives but amongst a myriad of multi-hattedness gleeful representation. I was platformed, facilitated and given freedom to express the multitude of frustration; verging on anger and not hiding my angst at what has befallen me since my accident. In truth, I was celebrated in being an emotional woman. And I was seen in my vulnerability and protected there. Now, I couldn't tell you if I was performatively demonstrating that openness as that requires an externalised position of self-reflexivity – a freedom only often afforded to the psychologically entitled. Like a comfort zone. But this deep dive into pleasure activism yielded a truth that had begun in the Victoria and Albert Museum.

That androgyny is racist: it centralises the white fragile beauty standards by which I was denied my femininity, because of the irrational preference for women to be hairless. There are many reasons why the capitalist patriarchy would weave the myth around hygiene and provide whole industries to cater to a consumer demand it ultimately created – this is covered somewhat in *The Beauty Myth*. But it succeeds in the art of capture, distillation and denigration of the variety in half of the population down to a tokenistic way of being, seeing and acting. One that I never was afforded the luxury of learning by osmosis as my peers seemed to, and then was further othered from by the off-white colour of my complexion.

My first act of tween post-trauma agency was to cut my hair. I had succumbed to experimenting with leg and armpit shaving and the occasional eyebrow wax; nominally because I wanted to fit in. But in turn could not bring myself to get the hair on my top lip removed or bleached. I to this day cannot explain that baseline. I wanted to slide under the radar after being singled out and told that my body, my pleasure was dangerous whilst I was still an innocent. I wanted a course charted and a way of navigating the world and how I was perceived that would feel safe enough for me to turn inwards to heal rather than having to externalise, vocalise and give in order to receive. That process did not come, and so began a decade of pushing at the margins until I exploded into technicolour in Dublin and then found myself in front of a mannequin in the exhibition *Making Her Self Up* almost sobbing at the sight of femininity incarnate – the wardrobe of Frida Kahlo.

I was fortunate enough to go see the exhibition twice. Once was a failed date situation and the latter part of the feeding my soul process that my social care budget has been the lifeblood of. It was a truly intimate portrayal of a fascinating, chaotic and deeply sensual creature. Whose sense of agency overcame childhood impairment, social positioning and gender turmoil even beyond death when private letters and outfits were stored locked away until years after she was gone from this world. Where plaster casts and devotee paintings, outfits and cultural relics mixed with what she needed to get through the day including a boot with a height difference and a non-stereotypical medicinal cabinet.

Months, a trip to California and a hate crime later; I feel resolute in saying that I am no longer protected by whiteness. Yellow fever is a lot more prevalent over here in the States as their relationship to Asia pulls from a different geographical location and is not so intrinsically linked to Empire as it is in the UK. I get mistaken for Latino looks-wise and often Australian accent-wise. Both amuse me although sometimes irritate and I am learning to accept the curiosity about my ambivalent placing as a compliment. There is a power in not being fit into a box and Frida to me exemplifies that. She chose her own. And should she have been in a country that was not already exoticised/colonised by the White Male gaze… then perhaps she would have had a similar journey as me.

I do not have all the answers of how to undo the damage done to my childhood self and the disgust I hold around what it means to be curvy, feminine and worthy of being cherished. But I believe I have made progress. I feel calmer, softer and more able to centre my comfort above all else. There is a long way to go to extricate my thoughts (my emotional labour/labour) for myself and my own processing but this piece marks a signpost in that. I am learning to forgive myself for my efforts to shame and deem myself wholly responsible for everything that happened to me as a safety net. I feel more able to seek solace amongst those I am socialised amongst and to see the value in truly saying #metoo. But the nuance for me to fully come home to my womanhood is not quite there yet; but I feel it – it is there on the horizon, a rainbow away.

Gender
by Hidden Ink Child

I have consistently found it difficult to describe gender and my relationship to it with words. Even trying to write something for this book, I stalled and struggled and eventually found visual art a better way to explain. I created these drawings in part to represent the abstract nature of gender, how little sense it makes to me when I really think about it and the arbitrary concepts ascribed to certain genders. This in particular applies to the expectations around gender roles. I struggle to grasp why we have certain expectations of certain genders in western culture, why some things are 'allowed' and others are not. These historically have also changed over time, which only serve to make them even more arbitrary. Each image here reflects a way in which I experience gender and its often complex nuances and feelings.

transbareall

Gender 1

by Hidden Ink Child

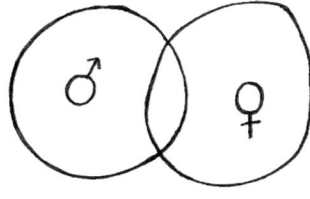

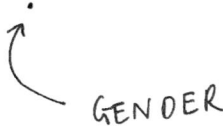
GENDER

Gender 2
by Hidden Ink Child

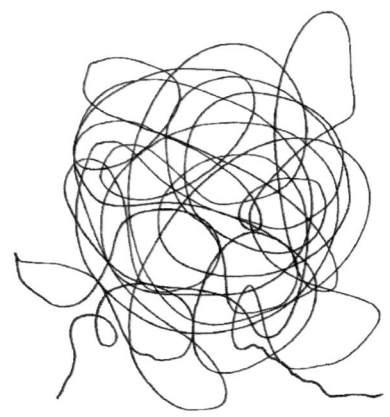

transbareall

Gender 3
by Hidden Ink Child

GENDER

GENDER

HIC

Gender 4

by Hidden Ink Child

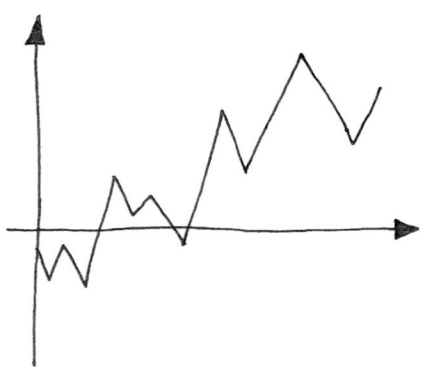

GENDER

transbareall

Gender 5

by Hidden Ink Child

GENDER

Saluting the Sun
By Roadmap Zach

I keep telling my thoughts not to kill me:

'Some people see me -
and that's enough.'
Existence can be tough.

All you're searching for is love.
But there are people who find my self-expression uncomfortable.
      They think my life will turn to rubble.

There are people that feel my identity is inconvenient.

My dreams are resilient.
My brain is hazy
      and my hands and body are lazy
arms upstretched, saluting the sun.
Mind silenced.

The end of the run.

I keep telling my thoughts not to kill me.

Suggestions
By Danielle Hopkins

Can I humbly suggest that you hate yourself?
Can I humbly suggest that you show yourself the door?
Can I humbly suggest that you leave your ego there?
Can I humbly?

Can I humbly suggest that you face your greatest fears?
Can I humbly suggest that you wear your battle scars?
Can I humbly suggest that you breakdown the walls?
Can I humbly?

Can I humbly suggest that you overcome poverty?
Can I humbly suggest that you overcome yourself?
Can I humbly suggest that you break all the conventions?
Can I humbly?

Can I humbly suggest that you be who you are meant to be?
Can I humbly suggest that you let others go?
Can I humbly suggest that I know what I talk about?
Can I humbly?

Can I humbly suggest that you lose everything?
Can I humbly suggest that you are not so well?
Can I humbly suggest that you change your body?
Can I humbly?

Can I humbly suggest that I get inside your head?
Can I humbly suggest that I eat all of your strength?
Can I humbly suggest that I spur on your dysphoria?
Can I humbly?
Can I humbly?

Un-male me
By Ms Mocha Slessor-Parks (MichaelShe)

Body 'un-male' me
Let true inner be
Un-shell, un-chain, release,
Set troubled two-spirit at ease.

Street's social shackle,
All my life's tackle,
Eluding tangled tongues,
And pointy finger prongs

Life's jumble tussle,
Mixed pieces in puzzle,
Odds yet to defy,
Wings to 'she' I fly.

Let heart's rose bloom,
Shatter trap of gloom,
Blossom through,
Live my true.

Oh my she,
Come to be,
From 'he' I flee,
At last be she,
A crown of glee.

Frank Duffy

Revolutionary Love
By Nathan Gale

I love trans bodies
Our scarred, compressed, repressed, incongruous bodies
They are authentic, and hot, and wet, and deep

I love crip bodies
Our strange, impaired, repaired, dysfunctional bodies
They are awakened, and hot, and wet, and real

To love a body as judged and unacceptable as mine
To want a body as desexualised as mine
Is an act of defiance
Our love, our lust, our sex
Revolutionary

But sometimes I just want to fuck!
Can we ever be lovers?
Or will I always be relegated to activist?

Perhaps, but then I've been called brave for taking my shirt off
    in public
I've been told I'm an inspiration for going to the pub for a
    drink with my friends
So it is perhaps not surprising that people think it's a political
    statement
for me to love a body that looks like mine
Because who would desire a body like this?

Well, in that case I really love activism
Our scarred, impaired, repaired, dysfunctional activism
It is authentic, and hot, and wet, and deep

Frank Duffy

Hearts and Nets
By BJ Christie

Sam Jackson pulled back his arm and flung the remains of his milkshake away, watching with grim satisfaction as the carton hit the street sign, strawberry vomit obliterating half the words. He shrugged his jacket closer and toyed with the idea of nipping back for another burger, but he was down to his last £1.95 in change, and he needed that for the bus. These days it seemed like he wasn't just living on the poverty-line, but dancing right over the fucking edge. Not to worry, though; Danny Mac owed him ten quid from last night.

'What d'you need it for?'

Danny shrugged. 'Just... You know.' Danny dragged his fag along the pub wall, and after testing it for embers, put it in his pocket for later.

'If you're after a bit of action, then you won't get much for a tenner.' He dangled the money just out of Danny's reach, enjoying the deepening of the other man's blush. 'More likely to get crabs at that price.'

'Not everything has to be about sex,' Danny snapped, the colour in his face rushing up to the tips of his funny, curled over ears.

Sam handed over the money, shaking his head. Sometimes, Danny Mac was a complete and utter mystery. He was probably the only person on the whole estate over the age of twelve that was still a virgin. How he'd managed to hang on to that particular item for twenty five years had been a standing joke in the Gladiator before some brainless wanker burned it down. Back in the day, two halves of lager and a bag of chips got you just about anything you wanted in that place if you weren't too fussy about where it'd been.

Trotting towards the row of council kennels where Danny lived, Sam winced. The McNeil front garden looked like a jumble-sale in a mental home. He hammered on the front door, ignoring the bell. The day he'd run across one wired up to a car battery had taught him all he needed to know about doorbells on this estate.

Mrs. McNeil looked him up and down through a crack in the door no wider than her lips. 'Yes?'

Sam's hand shot out. With a brisk shove, the door flew open and Mrs. Mac staggered back, the door handle cracking against cheap wallpaper.

Sam stepped inside the hall and kicked the door closed behind him, smirking.

'Where's Danny?' He demanded, Doc Martens crowding her fluffy Marks and Sparks' slip-ons.

'I don't know; I'm not his social secretary!'

He jabbed a finger. 'Danny-boy owes me money.' Pushing past her indignant clucking, he helped himself to the kitchen and straddled a chair as Mrs Mac eyed him across the remains of a fried supper. The sharp smell of grease reminded him that anything that could be eaten in three bites and washed down with strawberry flavoured snot couldn't be classed as a meal.

He took out a roll-up and sparked it without asking permission.

'Must you?'

He grinned and blew smoke out through his teeth. 'Yep,' he said, putting the match out in a blob of ketchup. He wondered if she was frightened of him. Most people were; especially the old ones. It was the haircut and boots that did it.

'I know you,' she said at last. 'You were kicked out of Danny's school.'

Sam winked, taking a deep drag. No-one gave you any shit when they could see scars through your haircut. Add a tattoo to the whole look and you were sorted. He liked that.

He was disappointed to see her disapproving expression change.

'What?'

'I used to know your mother.'

A silver-bright thrill of distress sliced through him. Teeth bit down hard on the tip of his cigarette, tobacco spilling bitter flakes on his tongue.

'She used to knock about down the Fold. Worked in the veg shop, from what I can remember. I never took to the new people.' She cocked her head at him. 'I did hear the owner was done for mucky videos in the end.'

She leaned forward on her elbows.

Sam squinted, the smoke from his ciggie making his eyes water. 'And?'

'Never mind; I don't expect it'll be there much after Christmas. It's all badly-spelled notices in the window one minute, and boarded up the next. You see much of your mum, nowadays?'

Sam blinked the sting out of his eyes, unbalanced by the sudden change of subject.

'You're nosy for an old bag, aren't you?'

Mrs. Mac smiled, seemingly unoffended. 'Well, I don't get out much. Not since my hip. There is the Ring and Ride, but it's a bit of a fag, booking it up. How are you supposed to know where you want to go, the day before? So do you see her about, then?'

'None of your beeswax.' He trailed smoke out between his teeth.

'I wish you wouldn't do that in here.'

He took another drag, deliberately aiming it at her.

Coughing, she flapped her hand. 'I'm asthmatic, you know.'

The kitchen clocked ticked loudly. Sam gazed about the room, deliberately ignoring her. Looked like Mrs. Mac was as talented with interior decor as she was with gardening. Less so, if floral curtains over filthy nets were her idea of good taste.

'Shall we chat while we wait?'

'About?'

'I like to get to know my son's friends.' She smiled. 'Humour me.'

'Why should I?'

'Because I'm old and smell of bacon?'

Sam hid the unexpected smile with another scowl.

Danny's mum cocked her head, looking like some scrawny old budgie wrapped in terry-towelling.

'The girls and I used to play this up at the Centre. At coffee-mornings, you know. Doreen invented it. Said she got the idea from her daughter who did an evening class. Introduction to Counselling, I think it was.' She frowned. 'Or was it yoga?'

Sam sighed. He pulled hard on his cigarette, blowing it out in a harsh stream in her face. 'Make your fucking point.' He stared, daring her to make an issue of either smoke or language.

'Well; I ask questions and you have to give me your answers without stopping to think.'

Sam frowned. 'Why?'

She smiled. 'It's fun.'

He blew another lungful at her. The old girl was obviously barking. He shrugged. 'Knock yourself out.'

Settling herself more comfortably, she folded her arms. 'Do you prefer motor racing or horse racing?'

'Motor.'

'Balti or Chinese?'

'Chinese.' He was suddenly hungry again. That burger had barely touched the edges. He wondered if he could make her cook him a fry-up.

'Pajamas or shorts?'

He grinned and shook his head. 'Bollock naked, me.'

'I see.'

'Get off on that, do you?'

'I might.'

Her expression didn't change when she said that, and Sam pulled a face. 'Fuck...' The edge of her mouth twitched.

'Stephen King or James Herbert?'

'I dunno... What d'you want to know this shit for?'

'It's part of the game. Nothing to be afraid of.'

He snorted. 'You don't frighten me.'

She cocked her head to the other side. 'So you don't read?'

'Waste of time.'

'Okay.' She looked across to the window for a moment. 'Preferred footwear?'

That was easy. 'Docs.'

'Favourite soft toy?'

Sam shook his head. 'What makes you think I had one?'

'Everybody had one. Don't spoil the game.'

He sighed. She was really starting to get on his tits. 'A rabbit, okay? Called Peter, with floppy ears and a red nose.'

He blinked in surprise, amazed at the words that spilled out of his mouth. It had been years since he'd thought about Peter; and he'd have bet his left nut he'd never have admitted to owning such a thing as a fluffy blue rabbit two minutes ago. He nearly smiled, but for the still sharp memory of Peter on the bonfire. Of struggling and screaming against his father's hands as the soft blue fur disappeared, eaten by the flames, the bright button eyes the last thing to go. He had dug the glass blobs out of the ash with a stick the next day, but mum wouldn't let him keep even those spoiled trophies.

'Yoghurt – smooth or bits?'

Sam cleared his throat. 'Um… I dunno. Bits, I suppose.'

'Sunshine or snow?'

A sigh. 'Snow.'

'Left or right hand to wipe?'

He pulled a face. 'Fuck, woman! That's disgusting! You're sick.'

She held a finger up. 'You're supposed to just answer. Without thinking about it, mind.'

God, this was Danny's mother. Was she on pills, or something? Forget everything he'd ever said about Danny being a freak, she made that skinny tosser look positively fucking normal.

'Lager or mild?'

He sighed, moving the dead match around in the sauce. 'Lager.' Five minutes. He'd give her another five minutes, then he'd bugger off down the pub, with or without Danny.

'Men or women?'

His head shot up. Predator eyes narrowed at him across the table. 'What the FUCK did you say?'

She shrugged. 'It's just a question. Does it bother you?' she asked, blinking slowly.

'Of course it fucking bothers me!'

She shrugged. 'I was just curious.'

He scowled. No wonder Danny was such a wanker, with this freak for a mum. He shook his head, disbelieving. 'Curious?'

She tilted her head. 'You know, considering.'

Saliva fled, leaving his tongue velcro'ed in his mouth. The cigarette burned down to his fingers, but he didn't feel any pain over the distant echo of his mum screaming at him, the familiar soundtrack of the past few years. He snatched his hand up at the sudden sting. He stamped, savagely grinding the nub-end into the lino.

'Mum?' Danny's voice called through from the hall. 'The chemist said you couldn't get that stuff without...' He walked into the kitchen, rummaging in a carrier bag. He looked up.

'Oh... Hi there.' He glanced from one to the other, unnerved by the brittle silence. 'What's up?'

'Sam just popped in to see you, love. Something about money?'

'Oh, yeah,' Danny said, reaching into his jeans. He held out a rumpled tenner, the note trembling gently between his fingers. 'Here...'

Sam suddenly shot to his feet, his thighs hitting the underside of the table hard enough to bruise.

'What's...' Danny reached out as his friend bolted for the hallway, bouncing off the doorframe - knocking over a Flamenco lamp with his unco-ordinated exit. The slam of the front door rattled the letterbox long after the lamp had finished its clumsy pirouette on to the carpet.

Through the kitchen window, Danny watched Sam run across Bells Lane, his bomber-jacket open, the orange lining an incongruously happy flash of colour.

'Oh dear,' said Mrs Mac.

Those two words told Danny all he needed to know. 'What did you say?'

His mother shrugged. 'Nothing.'

'Mum...'

She pouted a little.

Danny closed his eyes and sighed. His mother had a steel-trap mind and far too much time to brood. He knew he wasn't enough of a challenge for her any more. She made a little noise that admitted everything and nothing.

'Can't help yourself, can you?'

'It's a hard habit to break,' she admitted.

'What? Being a nosy cow?'

'Being a concerned mother.'

Danny stared through the grubby nets. 'Same thing – most of the time.' He gazed out of the window into the rain. It was starting to really come down now.

'You think he'll be okay?'

Danny's teeth worried at a snag of skin on his bottom lip. 'I don't know.'

'He's a bit angry just now.'

'He's always angry.'

'I know,' she said, turning back to the window. 'But you love him anyway.'

Danny smiled sadly through the nets. They could do with a good wash. Bung them in bleach they'd come up nice. Pity the same couldn't be said of people. Hearts and nets; casualties of too many greasy meals and a dirty world.

'I'll get over it,' he said at last, admitting everything and nothing.

His mother shook her head. 'I doubt it.'

There was no disappointment in her voice; no condemnation. He was grateful for that. Even if Sam wanted to punch his lights out for whatever had been said over fry-ups and formica, he'd get by because his mother didn't hold it against him for loving a man with a number-one haircut and a vagina. He supposed that had to be worth something.

He sighed, zipping his jacket back up. 'I have to go after him.'

'I know,' she said, and kissed him.

He closed the door quietly. He seriously doubted that Sam Jackson would ever learn to love himself, let alone anyone else. But that was okay. He'd take whatever was offered, be it anger or sullen indifference; it made no odds. Some people might say that was a strength, more would probably see it as a failing. But then again, who gave a shit about what anyone else thought in this grubby world?

transbareall

A bit on the side
By Annabelle May Hampton

A Midlands town, back alleyway, foggy, late evening, yellow neon light. A Russian built 650cc motorcycle, horizontally opposed engine, military-style sidecar. A prehistoric beast waiting for its keeper.

Make-up, stockings, dress etc. The helmeted figure throws the holdall into the sidecar. No-one will suspect, unlikely trip, unlikely transport, machismo preserved. Tickle the carbs, smell the petrol, six dead kicks, ignition on. A quick, sharp kick, the machine fires. Rev the throttle, leave it to tick over, three to four minutes at least. Depress clutch, boot it into first; the beast burbles gently as it edges towards the main road.

The Triumph must have been doing 70, it skids, narrowly missing the sidecar, a loose bungee and there lying in the road a holdall. The rider manages to stop and looks back. Leaving the bike ticking over he puts it on the side stand and runs quickly back to retrieve the holdall. A cursory nod to the fellow biker, the cargo bungeed back on, the Triumph rider speeds off into the night. The sidecar rider, about to continue, something catches his attention. In the gutter a size 9 patent stiletto...

Frank Duffy

Leaving Hibernation
By Rahil Cyril Virik

Echoed chirps from the roost pass on the secret warning:
I want to be seen, I want to be heard.
I cave my chest and wings inwards,
damaging myself so as not to bite you.
I am your hidden past, your hybrid future,
I am your saviour, your damnation,
I don't fear you, I don't need you.
Revealing myself only at dusk,
undetectable is the cost/adaptation for survival.
I won't break you apart, won't destroy you like you do me.

Your slurs and stares keep me hanging upside down.
Swallowing my fear, I peer down on the maze from above.
Just one way out, flap away from this enforced hibernation.
Enact echolocation, spread the sound waves for evolution –

We won't beg for equality, we have the right
We won't be in a corner, we are the core
We won't be erased, we travel time and space
We won't be seen, we are, we are

Previous page: Tree, Dreaming
by Connor Rose

A FAB Trans
By Lee Gale

Most of the time I love being trans. It's a great source of pride, of energy and of the creation of my most beautiful relationships. It has enabled me to live, to be happy and to laugh.

Sometimes I hate being trans, but not for the reasons I'm told I should. The media often tells me I should feel shame for who I am and disgust at my body, that I should hate who I was before or that I'm mentally ill or delusional. Instead, I sometimes hate it because I am invisible – my woman-ness has been wrenched away from me by others.

When I first started to transition, I tried so hard to claim a genderqueer or anything-but-wholly-female identity, but no-one understood that, including me, as I'd never seen much like it anywhere. I had one option open to me if I wanted to access medical intervention, which I desperately needed, and that was to tell the professionals that I was a man. I also started telling others, as I could explain that much more easily and I started to believe it myself, completely forgetting my genderqueer feelings and (potential) identity until I reread some of my notes from the gender clinic last year.

I now feel trapped on the other side of the binary where people can only see man or male. For many with a trans masculine experience or identity, that's perfect and exactly what's wanted, but that's not my experience or identity.

It's been slowly creeping up on me and yet I'm still reluctant to tell others, scared to use different pronouns (or unsure if they even fit – am I just conforming to other people's ideas of gender non-conformity?), worried about the impact on my partners (in case they fell in love with a man), or even to admit it fully to myself.

My masculinity in the way that our cis society would read it is only clothing-deep — because that's the floor or side of the shop that I buy my clothes from. I suppose what I'm trying to say is that I'm not a man. I'm not a woman either and I have no words to describe what that is for me. I think genderqueer comes the closest and I prefer that to non-binary. What I AM though is a being who has experienced societal female gender, of being read as a man, of doing things that are thought of as masculine and feminine, and relating to ALL of those things.

I could dress or express myself more androgynously, but that would be for other people's benefit — so they can see a fuller story of who I am inside. And that's not how I feel comfortable dressing. But am I also reluctant to do this as I know it's not as safe?

My woman-ness and my history and relationship to those experiences are still extremely important to me and really became more so as I was increasingly able to relax in my body. As I relaxed more into my body, my woman-ness slowly disappeared and now I'm excluded from spaces or even acknowledging experiences that have shaped me, that make me feel safe, that I understand in my bones because I've lived in those spaces too.

This makes me sad, and angry, and sad again. I understand the limits of the culture I live in (and angry again), and I stand aside to allow for women-only spaces as I will only be seen clothing-deep in those spaces. Ironically, trans-exclusionary people would claim that I'm female and always will be, but would be the first to chuck me out of their women-only spaces.

I feel a huge sense of loss, of invisibility and of other people's notions of gender being imposed on me. Of my own sense of self being stripped away and denied.

I know I'm not the only afab person who's read as a man, to feel like this. To those of you I want to say: I see you, I understand, and I love you deeply. And I want to acknowledge and send the same message of solidarity and love to all of you out there who are similarly stripped of who you are in this binary world.

transbareall

Cuddle Puddle
By Max Alexander

I ride the cuddle puddle wave
--a surfer who doesn't feel the wait--

the weight
of delicate flutters and deep strokes
fluctuates
but is constant

floating but tethered to tummies limbs fur dicks and other

trusting skin

I ride the cuddle puddle wave
it will break but nothing is broken
because the shores glitter with wide dopey eyes
reflecting and refracting
our newly explored waters

Fränk Duffy

Tight Lipped
By Remi Butler

    I scratch and bite
    I never feel quite right
    I claw and tug at all my wrongs
    They've bothered me for so long
    I've had to deal with them for years
    And carry around so many fears
    That if I show you who I am

    You'll just reject me
    For who I was.

Conversations with No One
By Benjen

Another oneofthose days, another dozen dozy hours scrolling through a stream of social media, selfies and cat memes, when you see another aimless clueless comment, casual in its antagonism. And it's Sandra or Helen or Susan or Liz because it's always one of those, and yeup Another grating comment.

Assholes are like opinions. Or however it goes.

'Too confusing! Why is it so important to label people? I don't understand'

2 h   Like   Reply

Sigh… I just. If something doesn't impact you at all Carol, why do you care? Let people have things. So I reply because I can't stand seeing this shit go unchallenged. I know how much it hurts me so I try and take it, a shield, a tank, protect the trans and queer folk who might also be seeing this, be feeling those same things I felt growing up, young, confused and queer. And I can't seem to stop myself.

'because now I don't feel so alone'

Just now Like   Reply

I want to leave it truthful but detached. I know my energy is wasted here, that too many times I've tried to appeal to people's sense of humanity to fight transphobia, to educate, to try and play nice and build bridges, only to simply get screen-capped and laughed at. To have my profile picture turned into a meme shared on a Reddit for 'trans trenders', to be doxxed, to be told to 'take a long walk off a short bridge', to be told I'm disgusting, I'm sick, I'm a pervert... unholy? Damned? Deserving death? For existing.

And I remember why I need to believe it's possible to beat this. So I reply again.

> Now I know that, it's not in my head, that there are other people who share my bewildering set of feelings. Gender. Queerness. That it's ok to let myself feel these things, that it's not just a "trend" or "attention seeking millennials" or "dangerous perverts" or any other of the vile dehumanising language spewed out when cis people talk about people like me. Who feel as I feel. Who's realities reflect my own. When government officials are debating whether or not people like me can use the bathroom or exist in public life, or be "unsuitable for children", or be something you should correct and medicate and pray away and.... Yeah. It's not all cis people who did those things, that's the minority, the violent and vocal and powerful minority. The most painful thing is knowing that most other cis people just watch it happen, just silently view the debates, and maybe if you know one of us you're wanting to help and trying to fight with

> us and that's good, we need that.
>
> But it's so difficult, to know that not enough people cared to stop it happening... How do you get back to a place of trust, from that?
>
> Just now Like   Reply

I hit enter. I know I won't even get a reply. No indignant protest, no bitter tirade, no pretence of 'debate'. Fucks sake, even those hellish little 'laugh react' faces would at least be some evidence of interaction. But no. It's ignored.

That's the problem with trying to engage with people online. You can put in a lot with no guarantee it'll ever be seen, or worse, be seen and immediately dismissed, forgotten. Leaving every interaction unsatisfying, and unfinished.

It's a foolish habit, one that's making me unwell.

If only I could talk like this face to face, but my words falter and my rage rises and I can't be rational or articulate or heartfelt because it's all I can do not to start screaming at them. Knowing if I did I'd lose my job, and most likely endanger any future jobs... So I adopt a politely neutral face. Trying to figure out if they know I'm one of the people they're so confidently brazenly abusing. If I 'pass'. Or if they know exactly what I am and know how trapped I am in my impotent fury.

I wish I had these words on my tongue. I wish I could.

Over: Cognisance
by Logan Turner

The Wilderness
by Louis Bailey

They say my gender is barren
a wasteland
they do not see its thriving
its life
the ecosystems upon ecosystems
buzzing, teeming
amidst the strife
and hardship
of a place, a space
on the edge.

They call my gender monochrome
but what fools are they!
They see not its colour –
the purple haze of heather
the orange glow of twilight
they see not the reflection of moon
on millstone
or the white streaks of early morning twite.

They fear my gender, dear kin
these folk in yonder village below
say it's too queer
but they don't know
like that foe of Devil's Elbow
that great, writhing mass of slither
I've always been here
listening to their blithering
ramping up their pitiful plight.

Previous page: Moor Man
by Louis Bailey

transbareall

I speak in tongues –
the cautionary tales of faery moss and bog
the slog and fog of the moors –
I shapeshift and descend
haunting their dreams at night.
My gender is unchartered territory
it exists on the map's edge
where there be monsters
glowing in the gaps between memory
glistening in its own peculiarity
residing in the land beyond
where the path gives way to track
where dots and dashes
and patches of Morse code
reside on the brink of time.

My gender is many lives lived
is centuries-old rings on the oldest oak
my gender, our genders, are evolving
like the whittling of trees into peat
the lick of fire and warmth of wood smoke
shifting with the seasons
restless, attuned
like the tidal pull of inward seas -
little capillaries of connection -
spilling over lichen skin
over sinew, flesh and stone
our genders are a wandering, people
our genders are returning
and a coming home.

transbareall

I Look Like A Farmer
by Apu

transbareall

the female king and the masterpiece
By MX Lupin

       In a world that rejects its own nature
                  e   n   e   i   g
       Forcing   m   a   d   r   n   essences into
       definite presences

       In a world that split   bodies meant to nurture
       Calling one a stifled him   Calling one a muted her

       Hiding the all-encompassing oneness, as the illusion of mixed
          messages

       A female king is rising,
       Unearthing,
       Seeing how skin still grows,
       When ripped off its labels used for illusive advertising
       Licking off false interpretations
       To heal to broadened perceptions

       But oh, oh the aching heart
       To see how many bodies, feel so far,
                   so far apart
       here come the clouds of comforting contingencies
       flesh suits watered as gardens
       creche boots, the young, the new army, suited soft where
          once hardened
       expressing beyond what false vision sees
       awakened to their living art

       He removes all constraints, his strengths no longer the weight
          on emotions, now a flowing rhythm

She unmasks, her emotions no longer the wet blanket to her
    strengths, now a flowing rhythm

beyond divisions no longer imprisoned he and she find
they. They find
steps in each other, not reps for competing
steps, back and forth, mismatches to inevitable meeting
their differences they find are more comfortable
when freed from the he and she as magnetic opposites, old
    ideas now fleeting
it is all a dance they see, all their pluses and minuses
there's so much more of them now they see, allowing their
    steps to intersect —
the female king knew this all along, never were they a still
    juxtaposition, with no room to interject
instead, just feeling things, in meaty things living via
    movement
encompassing endless steps for them, fluent moves entailing
    all,
the back and forth,
            the dives and leaps,
                        the jives and streaks,
    tickles and trudges,
                struts and swoops,
crawls and creeps,
all merging into one —
just one,
a masterpiece.

Non Binary
by Serkan Kasapoğlu

Make-up

I am traveling to Rome tomorrow with my best friend. Even though I am so excited, there is something in my head that keeps me thinking all day. Maybe I should talk with her about it.

Last night before Rome

'I don't know. I was drowned in thoughts again while I was alone last week. I think I want to restart taking hormones.'

'Why? You were quite certain that it was not what you want.'

'In fact, the progress I have made so far after starting taking hormones was exactly what I wanted. I was starting to look like I wished.'

'But your appearance hasn't changed since you stopped taking hormones.'

'I don't feel that way. I feel like I am going back all the way that I have came. Day by day, I feel less happy with my reflection in the mirror. Even though I was too ambivalent while taking hormones, I think I was quite happy with its effects on my appearance. I know that more femininity made me more free.'

'It's not necessary to take hormones to be more feminine. You know that my estrogen is higher than my testosterone but I always defined and expressed myself as masculine. No one sees

Previous page: A Continuum
by Ollie Scharaschkin

me as a feminine woman. Everybody sees me as a masculine person. Because I see and express myself that way. If you want to be more feminine and if you want to be seen that way, you don't need reinforcement. You just have to see and express yourself as you wish.'

'You may be right.'

First day in Rome

'God, this suitcase is too heavy.'

'Come on, you are a man; you can carry it.'

Third day in Rome

'You are such a cute guy.'

Fifth day in Rome

'Look! You will be like him in the future. Only with more make-up.'

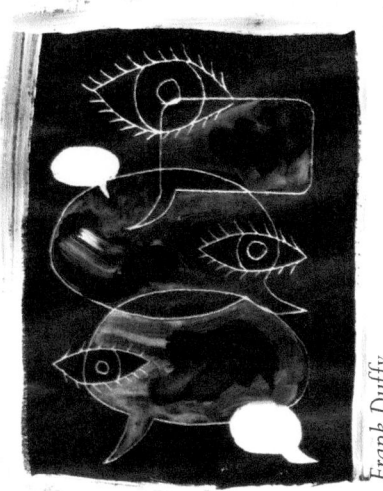

For a couple of years, I consult many different things to be the person I want to be. Hormones, or make-up, or clothing, etc. None of them was enough. Did I really know what I wanted? I always felt a lack in the way I left without knowing where I was going. When I thought I was doing the right thing, I faced obstacles, and stumbled. Why don't they just let me appear as I wish? Even my best friends are giving me what I fear most. Why don't they understand that my appearance does not determine my gender? Most of the time I want to be feminine, but I don't want to be a woman. Sometimes I want to be masculine, but I don't want to be a man.

Being seen as a man makes me feel uncomfortable while looking masculine, and the same thing applies to being seen as a woman as well. Even my friend who says that my appearance does not determine my gender sees me as a man just because I don't wear any makeup that day. Then, with the same breath, she says that I don't need to wear any make-up or take hormones to be seen as feminine. After such an inconsistency, everything she said the previous day was losing its significance. Now I don't know what to do. I want to wear make-up only because I want to. Not to make people understand that I am not a man.

Sonra neden başkalarının düşüncelerini bu kadar önemsediğimi soruyorlar. Çünkü başkalarının düşünceleri olmak istediğim gibi olmama izin vermiyor. Ne feminen olmama izin veriyorlar ne maskülen. Beni algılarındaki biçime sokmak için her şeyi yapıyorlar. Bense algılarındaki biçimden her çıkmaya çalıştığımda tökezliyorum.

Then they ask the reason why I care so much about others' thoughts. Because the thoughts of others do not allow me to be the way I want to be. They neither let me be feminine, nor masculine. They are doing everything they can to classify me in their binary perceptions. And I am stumbling every time I try to get out of those perceptions.

transbareall

Invested
by Crake Dakini

It started with my hair;
I began to see
that people viewed my body as their property.

They asked me why I'd cut it:
They'd preferred it long!
Everyone had an opinion, and my opinion was wrong.
I needed to remember that my hair was there for show,
an extension of my character, that I could style and grow.
Beliefs that I'd been harbouring about owning my own hair
Were met with outrage and confusion.
It was surely a delusion.
A sophistic confusion.
Or perhaps a mild contusion
that had put those thoughts in there.
They felt I'd done it to spite them,
that it showed I didn't care
about the value that they placed upon
my shining golden hair.

But this reaction was as nothing
to when my friends received the news
that as part of my transition
I had big plans re: my boobs.

And now I've seen true dedication
as people rush to have their say:
As they entreat and beg me
to leave my bosoms on display.
'You have such a great rack'
'A magnificent array'
The prospect of their loss has caused significant dismay.

But I have always hated them,
So I've actively repressed,
Any real acknowledgement
To myself about my breasts.
(I attempted to repress them,
But, at least, they're double D)
It is not a metaphor, to say that
They. Stand out. On. Me.
But as the years have trundled past,
I tried to do my best.
Tried to learn to live
with these great lumps upon my chest.
But suddenly I find
they're valued more than me!
People are so unimpressed
I want to live tit free.

But, I may have a solution,
for now it is my mission
to test their dedication
to thwarting my transition.

Since they're so invested
In my decolletage,
I will consider keeping it…
For a monthly charge.
If everyone invested,
paid a cumulative fee,
then I could keep my breasts:
They could rent them out, on me.

I should probably look into
all the back payments to date,
because I had no idea that up to now
I'd been so considerate.

It seems that hitherto
I've had no monopoly:
My breasts were never only mine
they're 'For humanity'
(Community chest, so to speak)

So, humanity can pay,
As if you're at the Tate,
And if you don't like it,
We'll both lump it.
That's my hourly rate.

transbareall

bridesmaids wait (1) - (they break their form below strange constellations, half-formed twisting on their point of origin)

By Beebee Vanunu

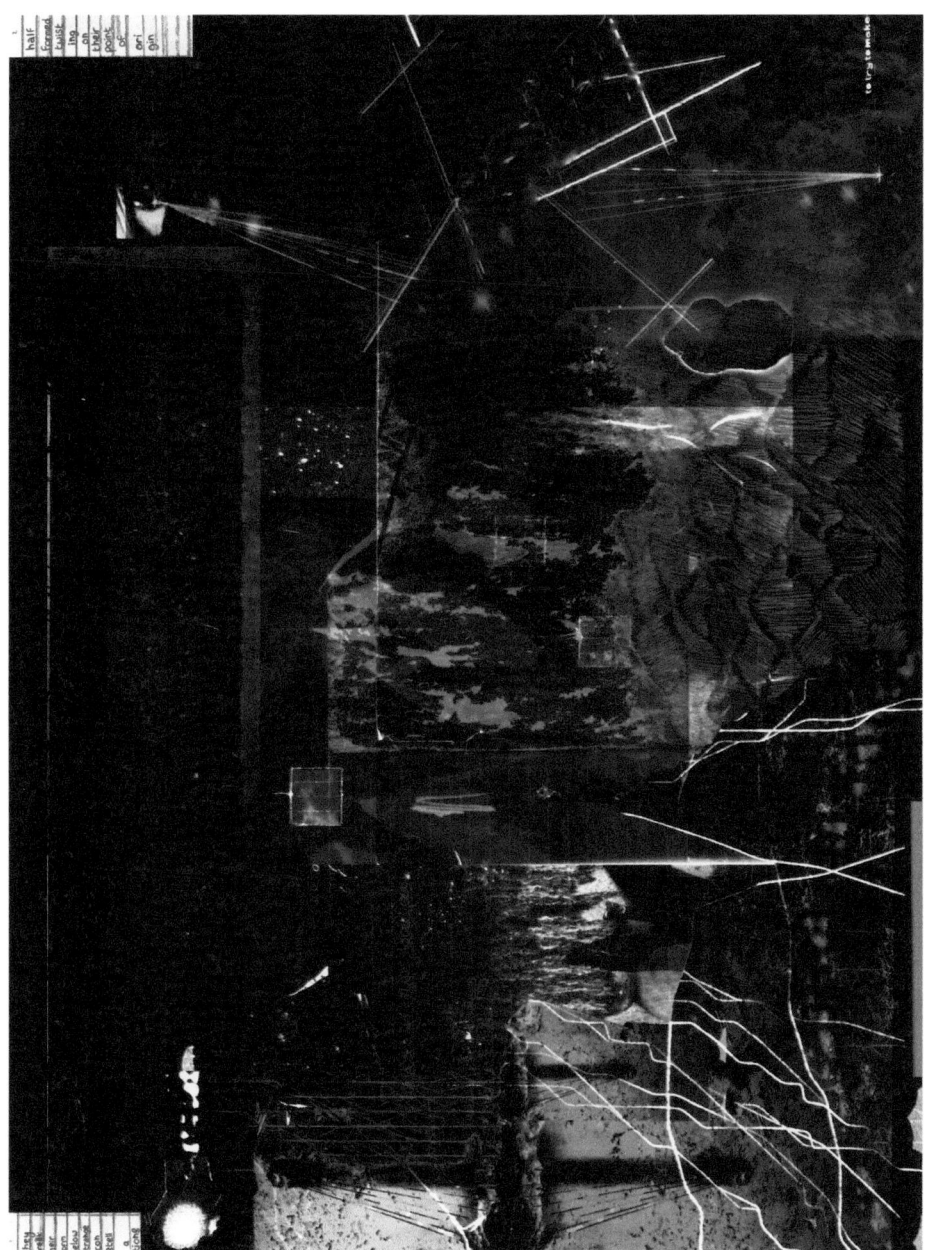

bridesmaids wait (2) - (and what a country! white hills, an accumulation of dust)
By Beebee Vanunu

bridesmaids wait (3) - (the dark's fire is an oil ground by gulphs of flame that burst reclaimed in pitch)
By Beebee Vanunu

Baggage claim
By Harry Robin Hunkin

I spent a lifetime
living out of a suitcase,
commuting back and forth
between places that weren't home.
I never stayed in one long enough
to bother lining my socks up in the drawer.

Every time, I waited in baggage claim
praying my case would show up on the carousel;
it had all the important parts of me in it.
It got so heavy
that the bite of carrying it around
lingers in aching shoulders and red welts
in the creases of my fingers. But emptying
it all out to toss away the things
that didn't fit me anymore,
would feel like losing.

The worst part was I didn't hate
either of the places I had to stay
or the things I knew I should
have thrown away a long time ago.
They just felt wrong.
The word 'home' was sour
on my tongue
but it wasn't poison.
The heaviness wasn't pain;
it was staticky numbness
like having pins and needles
in a part of myself I couldn't name.

Inevitably, things got forgotten in the hurry.

My toothbrush, my grasp on reality, my sun cream,
my sense of self, my comb.
They got left in faceless hotel rooms,
in taxis, in distant relatives' houses
until I found myself standing at border control,
not quite sure where I was going.
I didn't recognise the blank-faced photograph
in my passport anymore
or the name inscribed below it
and the gender marker was wrong.

You don't realise you've forgotten things
until it's too late to go back for them.
Standing in a white departures lounge,
that could be any departures lounge in the world
except for the variations in landscape beyond the runway,
the sinking something-forgotten feeling strikes.
The overpriced newsagent and electronics store
sneer at you and you find yourself wishing
someone had told you sooner -

'Don't forget your shampoo.'
'Don't forget that you don't have to carry around
the expectations of others
like suitcases full of cinderblocks
tied to your ankles.'

'Don't forget your plug adaptors.'
'Don't forget that you don't have to settle for settling
down somewhere that sounds like
an out-of-tune piano when you call it home.'

transbareall

'Don't forget to put your liquids in a clear plastic bag.'
'Don't forget that you don't need to cram everything you are
into only enough 100ml bottles
that they fit in a clear plastic bag.'

'Don't forget that you could leave the suitcase
on the carousel and remake yourself, undefined
by a luggage allowance.'

'Don't forget you don't have to choose between two places
when you could go to any departures lounge in the world
with never-before-seen landscapes beyond their runways.'

Don't forget the place you should be going home to is yourself.

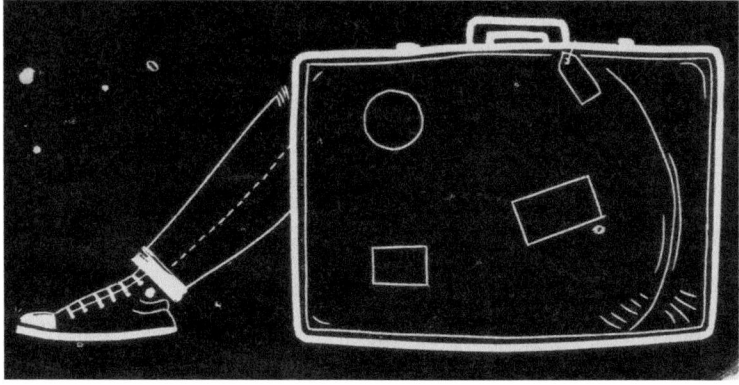

Frank Duffy

Dancing with(out) gender
By Robin Hob

Like many 'little girls' I was enrolled in ballet classes around the age of six. I can't remember much about them – what we did, what we wore, what the space looked like – but I remember two things: I really didn't want to be there, and we got a handful of smarties at the end of the class, though these didn't make up for how awful these classes were for me.

In many ways I had a privileged childhood regarding the room I was afforded to simply be. I doubt I was forced to go to those classes for very long. I can't remember. But those early ballet classes were the start of a rather complicated relationship with dancing. It wasn't the classes that I hated. It wasn't the first, second and third positions that made my skin crawl. It was the narratives that surrounded the idea of dancing. Dancing was something for girls. Thus, I needed to stay as clear away from it as possible.

I have often wondered what my childhood relationship with dancing would have been like if these messages had not been around; if dancing was not presented to me as being a gender-based activity. Would my desire to move, play, leap, slide, spin, twist, and boogie have been nurtured and developed? Or, what if I had an 'M' instead of an 'F' on that flimsy bit of paper that started a whole line of sex-defined identity documents? Would I have been able to form a relationship with dancing that afforded me more freedom? I imagine it would not have been as simple as my daydreams about 'what might have been'.

Through my adolescence, dancing and I didn't have much to do with each other. I had learnt that if I was to move through the world trying to convince others that I was a masculine-leaning person there were various things that were off limits to me. Any kind of interest in socially constructed Western 'feminine' interests would invalidate my claim to masculinity. These needed to be avoided at all costs!

My 20s offered me a new invitation to reassess my relationship with dancing as I moved to Wales for my undergrad and became quite involved in the dance music scene there. The house, breakbeat, techno and drum and bass scene in Wales during the noughties was male-heavy: a welcomed contrast to my undergrad lectures, where there was barely a male in sight.

These rooms, clubs, bedrooms and Welsh hills did not seem to prescribe that dancing was for girls. Dancing was for people. People who wanted to move, wanted to connect with others, wanted to feel the music in their bodies. Dancing was about being free. Moreover, dancing in these spaces, these male-heavy spaces, as a person who has a soft spot for cute, short, dark-haired, Welsh young men, was a playground for me. I was a minority in a sea of sweaty, dancing, shifting bodies; bodies who were looking for people with a body like mine.

My sexuality and physicality flourished in those spaces; with others, and also with myself. Dancing was a way for me to go inwards: close my eyes; feel the pulse through the air; the rise and drop of the sounds; to move with no script; to simply be with my senses. It was also a way for me to lean outwards: it connected me to community, to part of something bigger than myself, it helped me make new friends and lovers.

Those years in Wales, dancing in clubs, being in and with my own body, changed my relationship with dancing (and to some extent had an impact on how I saw my body too, or at least allowed me to see how my body could serve me, rather than it simply being an enemy). I was able to move past the lies I had been exposed to as a child, that told me that dancing was off limits to a person like me. I learnt that dancing doesn't care about gender, dancing offers an open invitation to those who wish to join it in its evolution.

The years went by and the places where I spent my time changed. As I moved away from late night weekends in dark hidden spaces, I tried to find new places where my body could play. I looked to jive, salsa, tap, ceilidhs and biodanza, and each involved their own limited, harmful, frustrating and offensive ways of bringing gender into dancing. Apparently, being interested in partner-based dancing means one wishes to reinforce the oppressive patriarchal systems of gender – no thanks, not for me. But even as I attempted to move away from partner-based dancing and explored biodanza (a form of circle-based dancing that is orientated around connecting as a group) I sometimes found that I spent more time sat on the edge of the room, rather than dancing with the circle. Sat out in silent protests against how gender was being performed and constructed. I stopped going.

Due to the career I have chosen (and had the privilege) to go into, I have spent the majority of my adult life in higher education, and I finally completed my required degrees in September 2016. I moved to London for a job I was excited to start and wondered if living in London, a city full of queers, might present a new chapter for me and dancing. I searched online for classes that might be open to a person like me. I found various queer/LGBTQ+ events, parties and shows; I could swim in the sea of queer dancing that was available. However, out of all those pages, links and lists of events, there was one group that stood out for me, but I questioned, yet again, whether they might be open to a person like me.

The Gay Men's Dance Company (GMDC) started about a year before I came across their site, and whilst I was drawn to email them asking, 'Can I come for a class?', I felt I had to pause first and question whether I was 'man enough' to qualify.

As a child I certainly felt more boy than girl, but like most of us, the boy/girl model was the only one that I was familiar with. I was desperate to be seen as a boy, but I also wonder now what was more important for me, to be seen as a boy, or to be seen as 'not girl'? My childhood gendered experiences were openly discussed within my family and other childhood contexts. But as a young adult I learnt that others (mainly boyfriends and some friends) found the subject of my gendered self a difficult topic to hear about, thus I learnt not to talk about it.

In 2011 I came across the concept of genderqueer as I immersed myself in the edited collection *Gender Outlaws: The Next Generation*. Excitedly, I started to speak to people I knew, letting them know that I had found a way to be in-between. Yet this was not met with any more understanding than my previous attempts to share my masculinity. 'Oh, OK, cool. Anyway, do you want to come to this women's film night on Thursday that we are going to?' they'd say. Fail! I quickly learnt that genderqueer was no easier for others to digest than my masculinity was.

Fast forward to September 2013 and I was moving again to start a further degree. Moreover, the pain of being read as female had been building over time and it felt like this was the right time to pursue physical transition. A year later testosterone took hold, my body changed and started to be read as male more often than female. I used 'he' pronouns in a lot of contexts, but I was also gradually gaining confidence in asking people to use 'they' for me, and I started talking about genderqueer again.

So how do I feel about my gender? Am I 'man enough' to go to an all-male space? When we talk about masculinity, what do we mean? A sense of self? A desire to be seen as a man? A craving to be seen as 'not woman'? The ability to access the social space of males? When I talk about genderqueer is it more of a political protest than an internal sense of gender? Or a solid feeling of not being at one of these two gendered poles? Are there times I feel more male, and others more genderqueer? If so, what does this look like? How would I know? Why would it change? Too many questions, and more.

I didn't know the answers to these questions in late 2016 before I emailed GMDC asking if I could go to a class, and I'm not sure if I could really give any better answers now. I may even give different, contradictory answers at different times. Gender is confusing, complicated and blooming heck, it's exhausting!

So, I went along to a class, and I have been dancing with them now for nearly two years. It's a relaxed, friendly, social space. We do styles from ballroom to Britney, salsa to Spice Girls, and more besides. I dance because I enjoy it, because I believe something happens to our spirit as we shift, slide and sway. I dance for connection with a group of men I hardly know, but once a week we come together as one. I dance because it hurts not to.

Despite this being a space that has 'men' in its name, it is the place in my life that gender has the least significance. I haven't talked to anyone there about my gender, my past or my pronouns. It doesn't really matter. I get changed with the other guys and the shadows of my history are visible on my skin. I am not sure if anyone knows what the two thin, pink, lines beneath my nipples say about my history, I don't know if anyone has even noticed, and I doubt anyone even cares.

When I had tried to do jive and salsa many years prior, I hated the fact that I would be assigned a particular role in relation to how others were reading my body. Now we will be placed in pairs in relation to size/height/weight. I am one of the smaller people in the group, so I will often be the one who is lifted, twirled, and led. Years ago, I hated this role. It was a role for girls; to be passive, to be led, to be protected, as that is what women need! But here gender does not determine whether I lead or follow, whether I lift or am lifted. And guess what, I love it! To be lifted and turned by a man with firm strong hands, with a big broad body and smile that says 'I've got ya!' makes me tingle and glow. It is not the act, the physicality or the moves, that is either loved or detested, it is the narratives behind the bodies that give these acts their meanings.

Dancing with GMDC has been an amazing experience for me over the last two years. I probably haven't gotten any better at dancing, but, in a way that I can't really explain, part of the wounds of my lost boyhood have been healed. I have found a space I can play, move, create, smile, shift, twist, stretch and dance without gender, in ways that were never available to that six-year-old who hated their ballet classes. I have found a home where the narratives others have about my body do not restrict the stories I can claim about my own body, choices and pleasures. I have found a group of men who have welcomed me, who have held me as I have taken risks, and who I have witnessed as they themselves have connected with aspects of their vulnerabilities. Together we make our collective stories about what it means to dance as men, dance as people – dancing with(out) gender.

transbareall

Transcape
by Annabelle May Hampton

A Letter to a Loved One
By Robin Prior

I didn't mean to hurt you.
It wasn't my intention.
Am I being selfish to not want this reflection?
If mirrors could see me the way I want to be,
They'd see a real man, a free man, me.

And I need to embrace my identity.

I didn't want to fail you,
To start this war,
So, before it hurts you even more,
I will go on this adventure and leave you alone.
I can no longer call this house my home.

I hate that I've caused you so much pain,
So, as I depart on this night train,
I'm writing to tell you that it has been true.
I have always loved you, even if you can't see,
That I am truly a man, not a woman, not a she.

I hope one day that we can be friends.
This doesn't have to be the end…

To Self...?
By Léo Taylor

Not all tread their own path in the beginning.
How fast others chide: we are not singing
from the same school song-sheet.

As our paths become our own, and intertwining
with other stars, emerging from winter, shining
we advance as one, in retreat.

We all know of the storm, through different eyes,
and we curse the rules, the hate, the lies
and yet…
still one last obsession to defeat.

Your permission.
The final leaf to fall away, at last,
unabashed and laid bare,
touches the still lake, and harmony swells.
Ripples touch all, and embrace.

The journey is a voyage at last. Complete.

Frank Duffy

Cracked Ribs
By Melody J Sproates

A chair and table with a piece of paper placed upon it. RUPERT, a man in his 40s, sits at the table, a pen in his hand hovering above the page.

MICHAEL, 16, stands behind him, just staring. He leans closer. And closer.

Rupert: Will you stop breathing down me ear like that!

Michael steps a few paces back, still eyeing the form. Pause.

Michael: So…?

Rupert: So what?

Michael: Are you going to…?

Rupert: Just give me a sec, alright! I haven't properly read it yet!

Michael: You've been staring at it for like ten years!

Rupert: Well this is just the type of thing that needs staring at for ten years, okay?

Michael: Just sign it!

Rupert: I can't. I just can't.

Michael: Dad, please.

Rupert: But they're your…

Michael: – Don't.

Silence.

Michael turns away. Rupert picks up the pen. Michael turns, eyes glaring. Rupert puts the pen down again.

Rupert: What would you like for tea?

Michael: Really?

Rupert: Yeah really, I'll need to get the shopping -

Michael: No. You're really asking me that question? Like right now? Are you serious?

Pause.

Rupert: …Fish and chips?

Michael: No! I don't want bloody fish and bloody chips!

Rupert: Oi, mind your language!

Michael: All I want is for you to…

He mimes scribbling on the form.

Michael: That's all.

Rupert: Can't we not just… buy something that would help?

Michael: Dad, this is different from asking for money, or a car, or a holiday. This is what I need.

Rupert: You *need* to give this more thought.

Michael: I have. This is what I must do to… survive.

Rupert: No. You need food and water to survive.

Michael: I'd rather starve!

Rupert: Darling, It's just not… right.

Michael: Dad, we've gone over this.

Rupert: It's important! It needs going over! It needs going over and over and over! There are other ways to feel happy, sweetheart.

Michael: I've never felt happy! Even as a kid, I just never felt… right.

Rupert: You've never felt happy?

Michael: Yes.

Rupert: Blackpool. Pepsi Max.

Michael: …What?

Rupert: Leeds festival. Metallica.

Michael: Dad...

Rupert: Or-fricking-Lando! We went on that bloody Jurassic Park ride six times!

Michael: That, that was a long time ago. It's different. I was happy, but-

Rupert: Yes. You were. All the Kinder eggs I used to buy you... The Doctor Who magazines... The collectable Pot Noodle temporary tattoos! Do you know how many Pot Noodles we went through in a week?! But you were adamant that they were what you wanted. And I accepted that. You were a happy child, because I made sure of it. I don't know how you dare say you've never been happy.

Michael: It's more of a... It lingers, and makes me feel... disconnected. From everything. You know when you've put on a T-shirt, and it's inside out. It doesn't look too different, you can just about get away with it. But it still feels... wrong.

Rupert: But your T-shirt is beautiful! It's colourful and bright and kind and clever and –

Michael: You don't understand.

Rupert: Okay. You're right. I don't understand. I don't, and that's why I can't let you do this. I raised you. You are my little girl and -

Michael: Stop.

Rupert: No. You really need to think about this. You're young, confused, going through a phase that may well pass in time. Shelley, honey, changing your body forever is not the answer. You wouldn't want to permanently damage yourself and regret it for a lifetime, would you?

Michael: My name is Michael.

Rupert: What?

Michael: I said my name is Michael and that is who I am!

Rupert: Honey… Now look, you're getting upset. You're only sixteen…

Michael: I'm nearly an adult.

Rupert: When you're growing up… You're going to experience different thoughts, different feelings. And when they come, you have to take time to

	live through them. There was a time when I was young, and I thought I fancied Jack Nicholson! But then I met your Mam and, y'know?
Michael:	Mam looks nothing like Jack Nicholson.
Rupert:	That not what I-
Michael:	Dad, this is different.
Rupert:	But Shell- honey, turning into a boy isn't going to solve all of your problems. It's not who you are!
Michael:	'Turning into a boy'. Dad, this is who I've always been!
Rupert:	For god's sake, they're your breasts!

Silence.

Michael:	Don't call them that.
Rupert:	I'm sorry, but you would be putting your body through unnecessary trauma.
Michael:	I'm scraping around in this dead vessel, dragged down to the ground by these huge lumps sewn onto my chest that are not supposed to be there!
Rupert:	I don't want to be held responsible for signing your body away. Have you even thought about this? Like, really thought about it? About your future?

Michael: I have thought about it every day since I was five. I have researched it. I've obsessed over it.

Dad, this is not my body. What you see, isn't who I am in my head. In my heart. I'm different on the inside. Like a kinder egg.

Rupert: What if you regret it? What if you wake up one day and just think – Shit. What have I done? What will other people say? Your friends? Teachers? You should be proud of the person you were born to be.

Michael: I am! I'm just... not that person yet. I want to be able to take my top off and... You know, I haven't been swimming in three years. Do you know that? I get dressed in the disabled toilets at school. I hide myself away from everyone. I just... I want to be able to take off this binder and experience life how I should be. As me. I'm sick of my crushed ribs and aching back. (Holds out the pen) You are helping me to be the person that I'm supposed to be.

Rupert looks at him. His hand quivers over the page. His fingers go limp and the pen drops to the floor.

Rupert: I feel like I'm losing my only daughter.

Michael looks at him.

Michael: But you're gaining a son.

He takes a deep breath and leaves the stage.

Rupert watches him leave and wipes his eyes. He sees the pen on the floor. He stares at it.

The end.

transbareall

B L U E

I stand among wildflowers
my hands finger them with open palms
w a l k i n g
trusting in their guidance
turning
       turning, as my family
on   and
   hands   knees
                pull them from the soil
but the roots are matted
and I am
     grounded
as I block out their murmurs of *weeds*

B E L L S

By Ben Hattingh

on the High Street in the sunshine
By Anonymous

Male. Masculine.
Maleness.
What is it to be a man?
Do you define gender?
Or
Does
Gender
Define
You?
Do you put on a particular show so that your mannerisms match the world's perception?
Or are you *you*?
Authentic in your own skin and stereotypes be damned!

I don't want to be the freak
The
Circus
Sideshow
[[[Look sweetheart! A girl with a beard!]]]
I'm as male as the next man.
My
Gender
Does
Not
Not
Not!
Define
Me.
I am male but so much more:
Spouse-parent-carer-sibling-child-gardener-musician-student-
          Mancunian.
So don't you fucking dare call me a girl with a beard.

Life on Earth
by Sez Thomasin (With thanks to Crake Dakini)

Of course, I can only speak for myself
But I have decided not to let you hurt me anymore
At least not with words.
Instead I will be David Attenborough
And simply observe.

You can rear up against me
Rasp your ugly thoughts into weapons on your tongue
Tip them with venom and spit
Say I'm unnatural, deluded,
A danger to children…
Say, if you like, that I'm jealous of men
Call my gender penis envy
Call my baggy jeans a costume
Say my binder is a lie.
You're only expressing your right to reply
And that's fair.
But it isn't me that your curled lip and narrowed eye
Are telling the world to beware.

But I'm not going to hate you
Because I will be David Attenborough
Calmly delighted
That you have shown me such a perfect display
Of your nature.

Don't bother with the get-out clauses
The false concern:
'I'm not being rude but…
Don't take this the wrong way but…
I just think you might be
Unwell

Mistaken
Too easily led
And perhaps you're confused
I mean, you do have a mental disability!
And didn't you tell me that you were abused?
How can you be sure that this gender thing isn't a symptom? A defect? A bruise?
I'm only trying to help...'

I won't try to attack or accuse
Instead
I will be David Attenborough
Fascinated:
'Look how this creature uses camouflage
To approach its prey!
But sadly, it's not very skillful
And will not be feeding its ego
On me. Not today.'

And no.
You don't have to use trigger warnings
Or content notes.
There's no law set in stone
In fact if you don't want to
Then it's better you don't
Because I'll take the hit
Of that unexpected
Rape joke
That unsolicited
Dick pic
Or that 'edgy' hot take
'There's no such thing as race, though!'

If they show me just who I'm dealing with.

And I'll be David Attenborough
Kindly explaining:
'Observe this display of dominance
This show of aggression
This strange little animal
Trying to give the impression
Of status and strength
In a way it's quite sweet.
This ridiculous insect believing
That I'm something it can defeat!'

Of course, I can only speak for myself
But I have decided not to let you hurt me anymore
At least not with words.
Instead I will be David Attenborough
And simply observe.

The things I am asked are not really important
By Frank Duffy

The things I am asked are not really important.

Would you like an icecream?

If I want the icecream (I always want the icecream!) I am asked: *vanilla or chocolate?*

Or maybe I am asked: *do you want an apple or a tangerine?*

These choices are big at the time but really they are only small because they don't last very long. If I want the apple today I could have the tangerine tomorrow.

Would you like to wear the red dress or the blue jeans?

I would like to wear the blue jeans

But tomorrow it is the school photograph so you must wear the red dress with the lace collar and the velvet ribbon

why?

I don't *want* to. It's not *fair*.

Goddamnit [deadname redacted] *I would like just one nice photo of you dressed like a girl is that too much to ask*

I never get asked if I would like to be a girl or a boy. I don't think I've ever been asked that, and that is quite a big choice really and it's important and I've never been asked it. Grownups seem to just think that's what I am but I didn't choose it and I don't know why they get to choose that for me. I don't know what it is that makes me a girl. I can't see it. Boys have willies but I don't see why that should make a difference. Maybe it's something invisible that only grownups can see.

It's *not fair*.

Sometimes I get asked about the stories I am told. *What do you think will happen to the little pig who built his house from straw? What about the little pig who built his house from bricks?*

I never get asked about why the wolf wants to eat the pigs.

I think maybe in this story it is just the way people think a wolf wants to be. Does the wolf mind that people think these things of it?

Let the Children Boogie
By Devon Bacso

Bowie blasting through lands of milk,
slow-moving animals swaying in the high grass.
Your hands on the wheel, my feet on the dash,
Kansas in the rear-view mirror.

Your face when the water bottle is empty.

The role of decoy:
My pale body slim, eyes wide,
hair long and girlgirlgirl.
Smile wide as the sun, trying
to send a glare so bright that no one will stare
as you enter behind me,
fingers tight around your tampon.

How you parade yourself, sliding on
the torn and worn
mask. Retreating back
into that old heavy body
as you chirp up your voice
and ask the way to the ladies',
the bathroom sign directly in your line of vision.

Then the explosion
your raised shoulders were waiting for,
as your hands scrub themselves clean in the sink.

This woman:
The coin purse of her mouth, how
her shoes squeak as she hurries out the door.
So frightened (a *man* in there)
of this simple body of yours.

transbareall

How she sees—maliciously and miraculously—
what you do,
on the days when you smile at your
self in the mirror.

I wait outside, eyes searching, exhaling
when I see you intact,
your feet rejoining mine.
The lines of the car glimmer as I finish off the gas, handle
kicking.

Hours stream away beneath our wheels.
You fiddle with the radio, bladder emptied,
fingers dancing up my arm to the bellow of your song.
I giggle into the safety of my shoulder,
one eye trained on you,
on the smile that flickers before each blink.

Later
my leg hums on the gas, head bobbing,
car velvet-footed.
I dart glances your way, soaking up
the stretched-out slackness of you.
The open peace of your sleeping mouth,
palm curved beneath your cheek.

The car purrs.
The doors are locked.
We're moving fast —
State line dancing
in the distance.

Next page: good timse bad splg

By Beebee Vanunu

transbareall

Identity

By Annabelle May Hampton

The structure of the end is complicated, he said.

The problem is the process of transition, he said.

The end is near, she said.

Call me by my name
By Ynda Jas

It's 4:51 AM
I've been fighting to update my name on a page
For the past five hours, almost nonstop
Coming up against the rigidity of Wikipedia editors
Or should I say, Wikicops?

Like the police
In a dispute between one of them
And an innocent civilian
They'll always favour their own
Won't listen to reason
Empathy lost
Defend the authorities at all costs

Discuss
Debate
Argue

They say to change my name on a page about an event in 2015
is to change the past
'We can't rewrite history to make one person happy'
'This is a matter of historical accuracy'

Well I'll tell you what's accurate:
Deadnaming can lead to
Gender dysphoria can lead to
Mental distress can lead to
Depression can lead to…
Worse.

And I'll tell you what's accurate
Throughout history I've been Ynda Jas

Simply known by a label of the past

Yet records are final
You rigidly rule
And for naming this violence
You paint me for a fool

Discuss
Debate
Argue
Cause lost

Call me by my name
Such a simple task

Call me by my name
Is it really so much to ask?

#wewillnotbeerased
By Harry Robin Hunkin

    I don't have to prove my existence to you.

    I refuse to explain myself
    to strangers who demand I defend
    my selfhood in essays
    of 10,000 words, double spaced,
    (yes this will be assessed).

    As if I only exist
    if I can verify it conclusively, irrefutably,
    citing scientific studies
    and peer-reviewed approval.
    As if without that, I am insubstantial,
    a hologram you could stick
    your fucking hand through.
    As if my existence
    is not proof of my existence.
    As if your response will be anything more
    than scribbled slurs in red marker
    over the neat black typeface anyway.

    So fuck your tests
    and fuck the way I was marked down
    for being pissed off that you made me take them
    in the fucking first place.

    I will write the proof of my existence
    in every chapter of my own story,
    in every second I spend laughing and loving
    defiantly.
    My existence is rebellion, my joy is protest
    and it will not be erased.

I will write love poetry to myself
across my skin in indelible ink.
I will tattoo the cursive letters into my body,
scar them into my flesh
until the conviction that resides
in the very core of myself
is reflected ineradicably on my surface.

I will write in blood and ash and charcoal,
scrawl the suppressed truths and untold stories
across every page of every history book.
I will write across the very fabric of time
by daring to survive upon it.
Graffiti on every space
I have deigned to fill, with
or without permission,
that I was here, I existed
in paint that doesn't scrub off.

I will write the rallying cries
that echo undampened throughout history,
telling the radical story of loving your uncensored self.
I will write the vivacity of myself across my skin
in every medium that cannot be erased.

Good Riddance: one Queer Jew's reaction to the toxic conflict between faith and queer identity

By Sahaf Hardouf

In an ongoing dispute between the Department for Education and a number of faith schools in the UK, a Haredi Jewish activist has threatened that many Haredim would rather leave the country than have their children taught about the LGBTQ+ community in a positive context.[1] The community, commonly referred to as Ultra-Orthodox Jews, is currently refusing to include any positive mention of queer people in its schools' curricula even though this is in violation of the Equality Act. The story as reported by Pink News was widely circulated on social media to retorts of 'Good riddance,' with some including more overt anti-semitic sentiments.

Such remarks do nothing to help the people at the heart of this issue: young queer Haredi Jews.

It is understandable that the first response of our community would be anger and that we would be better off if religious people who held bigoted beliefs just left us in peace. Many of us, myself included, have been cast out of communities, disowned by family and put through traumatic conversion 'therapies.' But, as we have been born into Haredi families in the past, we will continue to be born into Haredi families in the future. By reacting so flippantly with vapid comments of 'girl, bye' we forget the people whose lives would become exponentially more difficult if they left the UK.

The community's argument is that although they are tolerant of

---

1 Josh Jackman, *Ultra-religious Jewish families will 'leave UK over LGBT education'*, 2019 <www.pinknews.co.uk/2019/01/07/jewish-orthodox-uk-lgbt-education/> [accessed on 22 December 2019]

queer people, they do not want to promote our 'lifestyles.' For the most part in the UK, this is true and can be contrasted with parts of the Christian community that actively demonstrate at queer events. However, this is not the case in Israel where the religious community as a whole is becoming more conservative and wielding increasing power over mainstream society due to its collusion with Bibi's government. Only in 2016, a Haredi terrorist infiltrated Jerusalem Pride and stabbed several people in the Parade.[2] Israel is the most 'hospitable jurisdiction' to the Haredi community and this could be the future faced by young queer Haredim if uprooted by their families. In the face of this possible reality, should we really be saying 'don't let the door hit you on the way out'?

The retaliation against all mention of religion silences many queer people who also have a faith. In many circumstances, we are unable to fully embody our authentic selves in both faith spaces and queer spaces. For myself, my beliefs are the polar opposite of most 'religious' people, yet still, reactions to me speaking about my faith when meeting queer people are often met with scorn. When the only response from queer people to stories of religious bigotry is that 'religion needs to go,' it disavows many people's experiences of finding comfort and healing in their faith or spiritual practices. What needs to go is people dictating how others live their lives.

However, there is a growing movement accepting the

---

2 Yair Ettinger el al, *6 stabbed at Jerusalem Gay Pride Parade by ultra-Orthodox Jewish Assailant,* 2015 <www.haaretz.com/6-stabbed-at-jerusalem-gay-pride-parade-1.5381368> [accessed 22 December 2019]

LGBTQ+ community and many faith leaders are active allies encouraging other parts of society to be accepting. The senior Rabbi of Reform Judaism in the UK gave an impassioned plea for reforming gender recognition laws in support of her eldest child, who is non-binary.[3] She touches on interpretations of parts of the Torah that speak of a view of gender beyond the binary. This is by no means solely found in modern progressive movements as the Rabbis of the Talmud wrote of six genders, four more than most would expect. Even in conservative movements, dialogue with the LGBTQ+ community is promoting greater tolerance and understanding with the UK's Chief Rabbi producing guidance that Jewish schools should be supporting their queer students, which is a game-changer for the Orthodox community.[4]

This acceptance is not limited to the present day; the conflict between faith and queer identity forgets a history of gender diversity being celebrated by many different societies and spiritual traditions around the world. This is an inheritance that many non-binary and trans people are reclaiming, as it enriches both their gender identity and their connection to their cultures and ancestry. This history is either ignored or remains unknown to those who are so eager to fully destroy the opium of the masses. At worst, spiritual inheritance is

---

[3] Laura Janner-Klausner, *My child is trans. I feel blessed.*, 2018 <www.thejc.com/comment/comment/rabbi-laura-janner-klausner-transgender-child-1.470865> [accessed 22 December 2019]

[4] Judith Burns, *Chief Rabbi publishes first LGBT guide for orthodox schools*, 2018 <www.bbc.co.uk/news/education-45435583> [accessed 22 December 2019]

dismissed as backward and uncivilized. But by both fighting religious bigotry and celebrating the traditions and reforms that celebrate queer people, we provide space for all of us to coexist in our full authenticity. So, if there is one thing that should 'bugger off once and for all,' it really should be intolerance.

Good riddance!

Rehearsal *and* Space
By Franki Ayres (& paintings on following pages)

When I walked through the doors of arts and health charity Studio Upstairs as part of my recovery journey, someone said to me,

'So, you're going to make puppets?'

It wasn't a crazy idea – I did use to make puppets, plenty, brought a bundle to life on stage for a bunch of years as a theatre maker. My work has always been about transition in some form or another, merging bodies and boundaries with lives and stories that held them in – I made stuff! – as if for real!

This work, this time, was personal. Which is why I choose this piece to bare all, to you who might be interested? To you who might be with questions around your own transitions? Here are two images - the first and last from a piece of work titled Rehearsal Space.

In a deluge of appointments, torrential clinical!
to This letter, my body did not answer
as I had been led to make peace, back then, when
my first transition into a body fit to bleed again.
So I had to get out!
Out of my head
that's what I said…
then I said nothing else
and my hands did their best.

transbareall

In one day they made this first image, fixed on a piece of glass
for 1 month
while I waited…
with water, and expecting to leave some kind of hole behind
it surprised me how quickly the image left
how easy it was to clean the glass
to wash this piece away
until something else there lay,
and breathed,
all by its own accidental self.

transbareall

transbareall

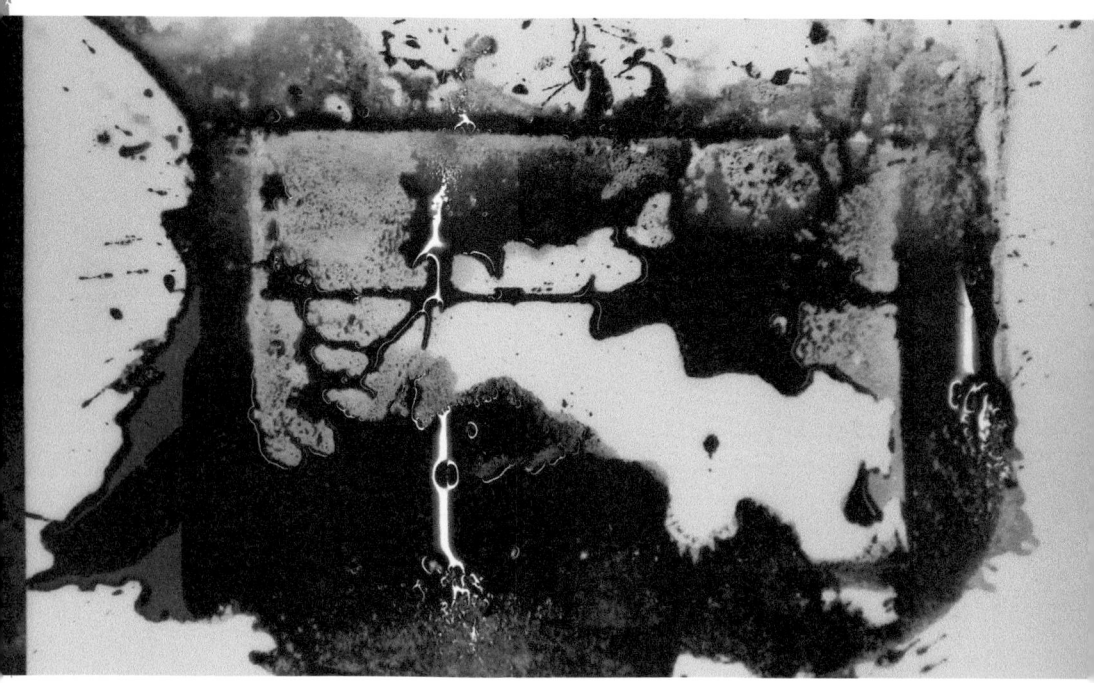

Gender and 'I'
By Sam Hill

Gender is an internal experience. My gender is my experience and mine alone, as is yours. I am not going to comment on the fact that you were assigned a biologically male body at birth and you identify as a man. Maybe you have never felt to question this. There is no judgment on your absence of enquiry, but I appreciate how our versions of reality differ.

I believe that concepts of masculinity and femininity are societal constructs and I guess you could say that I am an integration of these. Ownership of my Anima and Animus. I have two swirling energies that are dancing like leaves swept up in arms of the wind and the wind is the female base holding my maleness up – it's the platform from which I will rise. They are working together, not against. No patriarchy, no matriarchy, just synergy. I observe the world and on some level I believe we consist of our own cycles within a cyclical existence and that one element i.e. the masculine, cannot exist without the feminine and by way of one existing, the other comes into being and as the cycle meets, we are whole and one. It feels relevant to other cycles that many of us may not fully be mindful of or even that we take for granted - such as the seasons, life cycles, digestion, menstruation. Darkness and light. The binary is black and white, but what about the tones of grey? What about the dawn, twilight, then the fresh morning light of the sun rising, the bright midday light with short shadows, the warm dulcet light of the afternoon kissing the trees and rippling onto the earth, dipping light of dusk, the return to twilight again, solace of sunset, darkness, night-time and out come the stars – the speckles of light strewn across the blanket of darkness, together. Our whole existence is cyclical. The tones are non-binary and present and valid.

Frank Duffy

The movement of my entire existence feels like it's about integrating this darkness and the light, gender an aspect of this; it's my authentic way of being, knowing that I am made up of many parts, a spectrum. They are not separate but elemental to my whole, and in being full I can be empty, and when a vessel is empty it becomes useful. I think of the houses we live in, the cars we drive, even the bags we use being functional because of the space. Space is important, as emptiness is the core of everything. Not in the sense of desolation, although it's when I am sat in a desolate landscape in nature that I feel most connected to myself and to something far more expansive, yet there feels no separation – these are my times of peak experiences. There is flow within my stillness. I feel like water navigating through life, hitting rocks but adapting, transient in my shape and form as my cells die and regenerate and my moments dissolve as new moments are created, tides. Intense joy, profundity and unity.

In my younger years, I felt like there was an imbalance within, very little expression of the sun to my moon. Having experienced anxiety and depression and some very despairing times, I found that it was partly because I wasn't living my truth. I know my body well enough to listen to its dialogue of 'go this way instead,' and that it's ok to trust this. There is no such thing as a wrong choice. So I listened to my dissonance, my imbalance, and explored my childhood feelings. In therapy I explored the idea of being a man which didn't fit, and neither did the idea of being a woman: I am wholly both and wholly neither, which leads to that feeling of oneness. The biological sex of being a man is a characteristic but not necessarily an experience that is lived internally. Being a man doesn't mean you need to convey the masculine way of being that society expects and that we introject. You might feel quite 'feminine' internally. Why can't we be recognised as being both? Why is it important to have a male toilet and a female for our most human act of defecation, which upon analysis is neither male nor female itself and smells the same (Hi, I'm a man poo!). I think of Shakespeare – 'A rose by any other name would smell as sweet'! It's ok to feel how we feel and to own and validate our experiences. I'm learning more and more the value in just being, and not trying to justify myself to anyone anymore;

educate and share yes, but not justify. After all, if we strip away gender, there lies a universal and collective connection between all of humanity; experiencing fear, loss, joy, anger and love - regardless of our circumstances, regardless of our identity.

For me it isn't about being born in the 'wrong' body, as nothing is wrong. Wrong sounds negative, when all there ever really is, is what is. My body is my own. I have the freedom to express it as I wish and it is more about evolution and growth. I think back to being a child – that time of liberation, free from the shackles of labels, well… free from any understanding or true concept of them, a time of innocence and purity. It was my favourite time: hormones hadn't kicked in and I was just being me. I dressed in 'boys' clothes and I felt a connection to being a boy, an energy. I felt a connection to being a girl in other ways, again an energy. I didn't understand at that time and I didn't care - there was just momentum, and I soared. I wasn't concerned with gender, but was living in the moment and this is how I imagine being close to death might feel like too (again the cyclical nature presents itself). Yet to be afflicted by hormones; we all looked the same, smooth skinned boys, similar high voices. I wanted to cut my hair though. This act would be my reverse Samson and Delilah: by cutting my hair I was gaining strength in expression of who I was. It could have gone either way as a teenager, but it so happens that I was born into a female vessel, so testosterone was never going to be my dominant hormone and for this I would spend the next twenty odd years feeling inadequate and off kilter; self-deprecating, self-harming, flagellating, yet also finding myself and self-awareness. As a child it was most distressing when I started to develop breasts. I was losing the androgyny that made us all the same and I was entering another rite of passage. I was now going to be labelled as a woman based upon my sexual and physical characteristics and society would treat me in a certain way. How can we not be both male and female? When we are all born of man and woman, part mother, part father (whomever our creator is – it comes from these basic biological cells) our very conception involves the cycles of masculine and feminine uniting and I'm speaking of the masculine and feminine within.

My journey became about expressing my external in a more masculine way. It was about the relative, the here and now, and not the spiritual absoluteness of nothingness for me, yet it was also about this. It was about change, metamorphosis, with the core of who I am remaining unchanged. It was and it is about transience. I am following the thread, trusting what feels right and truly expressing who Sam really is. I feel that I would rather feminise my masculinity than masculinise my femininity: that's where I get my balance back. My intuition tells me I will feel some sense of balance physiologically, even though of course only the process will reveal this as being true. What I am certain of is that, by living authentically, the hormone cortisol (derived from the stress and anxiety of trying to fit into an existence that I can't claim as my own) will be reduced, and I will feel more grounded, not floating out of my body in a surreal state of dissociation. I will feel embodied. I have no doubt in this feeling liberating – and that in finally feeling connected to my body, I will also more freely let go of it, because how can you lose what you never had? I need to gain it to lose it, and fully embrace both life and death.

Despite feeling I have gone on a natural trajectory, I've been sitting in a liminal space for most of my life and am now following the path in the only way I can. I struggle with the fact that it is and can only be a synthetic way. An interesting paradox. I am pharmaceutically changing my physiology and physique to feel more 'me', and it's not free range testosterone milked from man (can you imagine?!). All I can do is trust in the fact that I am alive at a time that makes this possible: this journey is authentic to me in this time period. My essence remains, and so I consider all of this a part of my spiritual growth too. Accepting what is: I accept that I am in love with a female and I have no means to procreate with her apart from through the wonders of science. I accept that I am alive here and now and that this is what feels right, so I am being with what is and what science can allow. I accept that this is the liminal place of unrest that has felt monumental to growth and development; the discomfort leads to introspection. By harvesting my eggs to go through fertility treatment it feels like I am fulfilling the purpose of having a female body, my final act before I transition – I am choosing how to use my body more importantly.

The dark nights of the soul were all part of the realisation; it wasn't about repression and begging for the pain to end, it wasn't pushing it out of the room, it was about the experiencing and the shedding from movement, the dance of development. I think we all deserve the choice in what happens to our body. That's why I feel so strongly about the choices we can make as we are dying: where our body resides, what medication we have, when we say we have had enough. I embrace the love I feel from my heart but one day my heart will stop beating and I may choose for it not to be restarted. I will let go, I won't be attached to living anymore and I should set the boundaries. We may try to spend all our lives living as our most authentic selves, or trying to in a society that is often trying to mould us into something more generic, when actually we are the unique tones. So why can't we die in this way? A death fitting to the individual and then as we die, we let go of the ego, let go of 'I', let it dissolve into the ether and be at one. As we grow old and closer to death our physical self becomes genderless: women lose their periods, men become impotent and so the biological characteristics of what made us a 'man' or a 'woman' are no longer defining. We also look more androgynous too, like when we were a baby. As we die we revert back to needing care, and in vulnerability we return to innocence, how beautiful surrender will feel. How ethereal.

Gender diversity and androgyny is not a modern concept, it is not a fashion statement. It is etched across history and culture. An expression of masculinity/femininity doesn't take away from being a specific gender if you look at the world in this way. Tapping into the cycle or spectrum of gender tones isn't taking away from, it's adding to. We are delicious and wholesome, we are all beautiful. Language is also unimportant for me. I appreciate its value in helping us derive meaning and to understand the world, as categorisation helps our human brains to process. It's evolution, it's survival. It is understandably important for some in order to be 'seen'. However well language serves us, it can also limit us – it can negate the fact that gender is merely a part of a multi-faceted person. The holistic person somehow gets lost in being objectified by language and the stare of others; why not let the stare become a gaze derived from experiencing everything that can be seen of a person externally but also beyond this, the invisible but perceivable. We might not be able to see our beautiful heart that lies in darkness, but it's there. Everything in its entirety, moving from objectification to relation.

I want to be experienced as a whole, related to as a whole - it's not about my gender, it's not about my sexuality, my queerness, not about my skin colour, hair colour, my job, my interests, my introversion, my veganism: it's about all of this in the moment, existing at once, it's about more than what can be quantified and witnessed. It is feeling, it is essence, and it is beyond 'I'.

transbareall

transbareall

Kim

by Allie Crewe

The Strawman
By Kira Nelson

Have you heard the Straw Man call?
He's small but stands with giant friends
Lies and slander shape his world
Cuts down the different to meet his ends
He seeks to define me by the tumour that binds me
By my flat chest, not-grown breasts
The prison that confines me
Our struggles and our pain he deems mild
Speaks not of loving parent but tortured child
Condemns our silence and ignores the speaker
Protecting the weak by attacking the weaker
Oh, children weep and logic falls
When the cursed Straw Man calls

To woman and faith we pose a threat
All this inside the Straw Man's head
Hatred and violence called down from above
All in the name of a man who preached love
Freedom and expression he has named sin
But I will not let the Straw Man win
Gender resides not in body but in mind
This fact, not opinion, is one he shall find
Your soul will grow wings and you will fly far
If you dare to be different, and be who you are

More

[G]
What do you see
when you see me?
~~Does your curiosity~~
[D]   [G]
Do just see a man?
[G]
Cos I'm so much more

[G]   [G]
What do you think
when you see me?
       [D]
Does your curiosity
       [C]
leave you wanting [G] more?

And I'm so much more x4   [D] [C] [D] [C]

    [C]   [G] [G] [D]
I'm more than just a tabloid sell
    [C]   [G]   [D]
I'm more than just a story to tell
    [C]   [D]
I'm more than just the letter T
    [C]   [C]   [D]
I'm more than just diversity.

What do you do
when you see me?
Does that curiosity
burn through your mind

What do you ask
when you see me
I might be your first
but you're not mine

And I'm so much more x4

I'm more than being fetishized
I'm more than a woman disguised
I'm more than just a box to tick
There's more to being a man
than having a dick.

By Lee Gale and Jacob S

Floating World
By Leslie Tate

My eye is drawn to the wedge of sky
outlining this man.
His shaved head shows up like a rock.

In his mind,
the blue and white seascape canvas
seen from the cell of his bedroom
takes him on a journey.

It's all part of the novel he's writing.

He's cloud-riding Odin
looking down at a darkened corner
where his childhood used to be.

His dream's inside, navigating the floating world
of high cirrus and whited church towers
to live forever on cool air.

Caught between light and dark, he hears
the door closing on jet-stream memories,
sees from the past,
the tops of trees stretching to the sky.

Death has no Language
By Rami Yasir

Drunk, glass in hand, you've got that old hope
that this will be your last shot. Last shot. And again,
last shot. Blurry eyed, you stumble to the jukebox

wanting nostalgia like a drug, aching for something loose,
trying to relive those reveries of teenage years
where nothing made sense like music did. You find that one
        song

by Muse; you slur along. The notes hurt your throat;
English letters with sharp edges drawing blood
from your voicebox. It hurts. You don't stop.

~*~

This poem is about a club. A deep cesspit of sin, and proud of it.
The Underworld reeks of queer sex and gin. It sings
with dark lighting, dark skin. Maud

the old barwoman, wipes counters, watches you stumble,
shakes her head and ignores your tears. Another day,
another sorrow. She knows the feeling.

It's evening. The place isn't full, never is really, but right now
it's just you and Maud. You both take up space
near that wooden counter, opposite sides, a dark oak border

drawn between work and pleasure. It's hardly entertaining
to watch you stumble in hurt, to clean up the blood
you cough up with more liquor. She laughs anyway

because what can you do? She's not a cruel woman
but cruelty had her followed. It sat in the set of her shoulders,
at her neck, in the hollow, in the knowledge that the Earth still
      spun

when the world chewed her and swallowed. And if the world
is cruel, then the Underworld is Cruella. It makes coats out of
      skin,
weaves thread from melanin, makes the best of a bad situation

and stitches it all into drag that screams:
I am here to be seen.
But you'd rather speak than be seen.

Maud transitioned late, pushing sixty, she's on HRT,
takes oestrogen. You could map her body on a timeline
of terror, then power, then back again. Maud had a wife

bought her dresses in secret, faux-pearls and eyeliner.
You wouldn't believe how much change a little paint makes,
how hard it is to find foundation in her shade. Maud aches.

She died, her wife. Aneurysm.
Here one day, gone tomorrow.
Maud stops cleaning.

Please stop your screaming, she calls from the counter.
Those sharp English letters latch onto her sorrow,
worry the wound of a fetid unknown.

Here, come here, she says, if you'll let me borrow
a moment of peace (how long?) then I'll tell you a story.
Like a mother sending her kids off to bed.

Maud has no children. She'd been scared of what it meant.
Maybe without them she was more lonely than with
bits of her blood made real. But in the end

they'd just die like the rest. Now listen, she says
as you lurch onto a barstool, have I told you the story
of how I was half blinded? You shake your head.

Well that's as good a place as any to begin.

~*~

The doctors say it's all in my head. I don't disagree
but that's not where it starts. I was working, back then
I had only just been hired. When Gayatri died, this job was
      good to me.

You meet people. It made me feel like something real again
to speak to someone other than God. That's not a complaint!
She directs her last comment upwards, Madonna comedienne,

then grins at you as you sway from right to left. She sighs. Your
      eyes
are dull and drooping, that bad song from the jukebox is
      looping,
repeating the same verses over again.

And then it all stops. And the quiet holds you both.
It cradles your foreheads like it could kiss your thoughts to
      sleep.
It allows the world to sing.

Cars rumble, people speak, the world moves and moves
and keeps moving. In the building above are a couple
about to split. They're long distance; it's too hard to keep doing
    this.

There's a difference between the ghosts of things you lost
and things you almost had, but here they sit
together, stroking your hair, telling you to breathe;

that every breath is a gift, every regret a reminder
that the world moves and moves and keeps moving. It's okay
to feel it like a knife between your ribs. It's okay

to remember the good things and feel like shit. Every breath
is a gift, yours to keep or get rid of. Yours to swallow
or use to speak. And Maud breathes. And you breathe.

In the momentary silence, the story bubbles. Maud can't bear
to leave it unspoken. For some reason it hurts more
unshaped and unsounded, like a bruise under the skin

of her second language. For some reason this quiet
is soothing, is music. For some reason her faith
in the story is bolstered. And you listen. Listen.

Words are only shapes until you speak.
Maud says a prayer,
lets her story fill back up, and leak.

Maud was never a young queer on the scene. She took this job
because after Gayatri it seemed pointless
to settle alone between the sofa cushions. The Underworld
    took her

because in the end we all die. So will she, one day,
and she can't do that alone. At least here
she can talk to her customers and colleagues.

Someone will miss her, at least. And maybe after,
she'll be with Gayatri again, and they can stay still together
between the sheets of the ozone layer.

She still has belief. Maybe not the same as before,
and she's not sure for what, or who, or why,
but she has it in something. She used to wish for more,

maybe then she could close her eyes and try
to die without fear. But that was a while ago,
before she started here. Still growing. She's proud of that.

Maud pauses to smile, then speaks.
Once there was a brown kid. Maud had just been hired,
had been cleaning counters for just about a week

when they arrived with bloodshot eyes, their back stooped and
    tired,
and sat at the bar with their head in their arms.
Get me drunk, they said, then said nothing else,

and Maud, being new, simply stared, bewildered.
Get me drunk, they repeated, you have to,
it's written. It's all a fiction, I'm going to end,

so get me drunk, stop my thoughts, pack my faith
in a bottle. Make it real, give it form,
then let me drink it.

transbareall

They sigh, then they laugh, then they sigh once more.
I'm sorry, they say, but my love's in a coma,
so please get me drunk, and let me forget

that endings are fake, that beginnings don't matter
that my talent is built from nylon and plastic
that from where I am death has no language.

Get me drunk, Maud, please. Let me forget
I made you to make me. I'm in my own debt.

Maud, stunned to silence, only nodded and picked
a bottle at random, a glass to pour it in
and watched as the brown kid drank like a fish.

Maud, they say, quiet and hard, if I take your sight
and make you a bard, Maud, will you sing of me?
Can I live through your words?

When my body is rotted and my soul is recycled,
will you keep me alive? Will you even try?
Will you make sure they find me? Will they know they're
    entitled

to the bits of me shaped in your soft hands, all my
fears laid bare, arranged in three lines?
I don't want to die, Maud. I'm too scared to try.

Get me drunk. Give me beer. Give me spirits and wine,
so I'll sing, and you can sing, and we'll make a harmony.
I'll leave you one eye and I'll take one with me.

Well? Says the kid, and they sound so tired,
so Maud takes their hand and speaks to the quiet.
I'll try, Maud says. I promise to try.

Half-blind faith. Half-bard, half-singer,
half-drunk, then full-drunk, then too drunk
to see. They passed out at the counter.

The next day Maud woke up blind in one eye.

~*~

That's the story, Maud sighs at your sleeping body.
The jukebox is silent. It rests like a weight
massaging the breath from your sleeping chest.

Things carry on. It's getting late. Rush starts soon,
but her shift ends at midnight. She might stay later.
There are more stories burnt into the wood of this counter,

in the sweat smell of her dark skin, in the hairs that reach
like supplicants from her arms. In the air she breathes
an alphabet in dust particles. The Underworld

sings with things left unspoken. She's not happy, not sad,
but her heart feels less broken.
Get me drunk, Maud sings softly,

in the dark of the club.

transbareall

Build Queer Resistance
by Apu

Queerling Bodies
By Daniel Morrison

Let me peel away the layers from your eyes, with mine.
The caution, curiosity, desire, until we stand, soul naked.
Let me be the first to kiss you
Holding your new name safe in my mouth.

Let's learn each other, treading gently on uncharted lands.
Give me beautiful men, freshly furred,
The heart and stomach of a king held softly in exquisite curves.
Meet me in the liminal spaces where bodies shift like sand.

Give me real genitals;
Detachable, retractable,
Deconstructed, reconstructed,
Renamed, reclaimed, unshamed.
Give me girl dicks and man cunts
And bodies unbinaried.

This is us, skin on skin, human,
Blood pulsing, fire rising, animal,
Hearts flaming, embers glowing, infinite.

We break our path with bare and bleeding hands
But we walk together.

Over: And through it all
by *Simon Williamson*

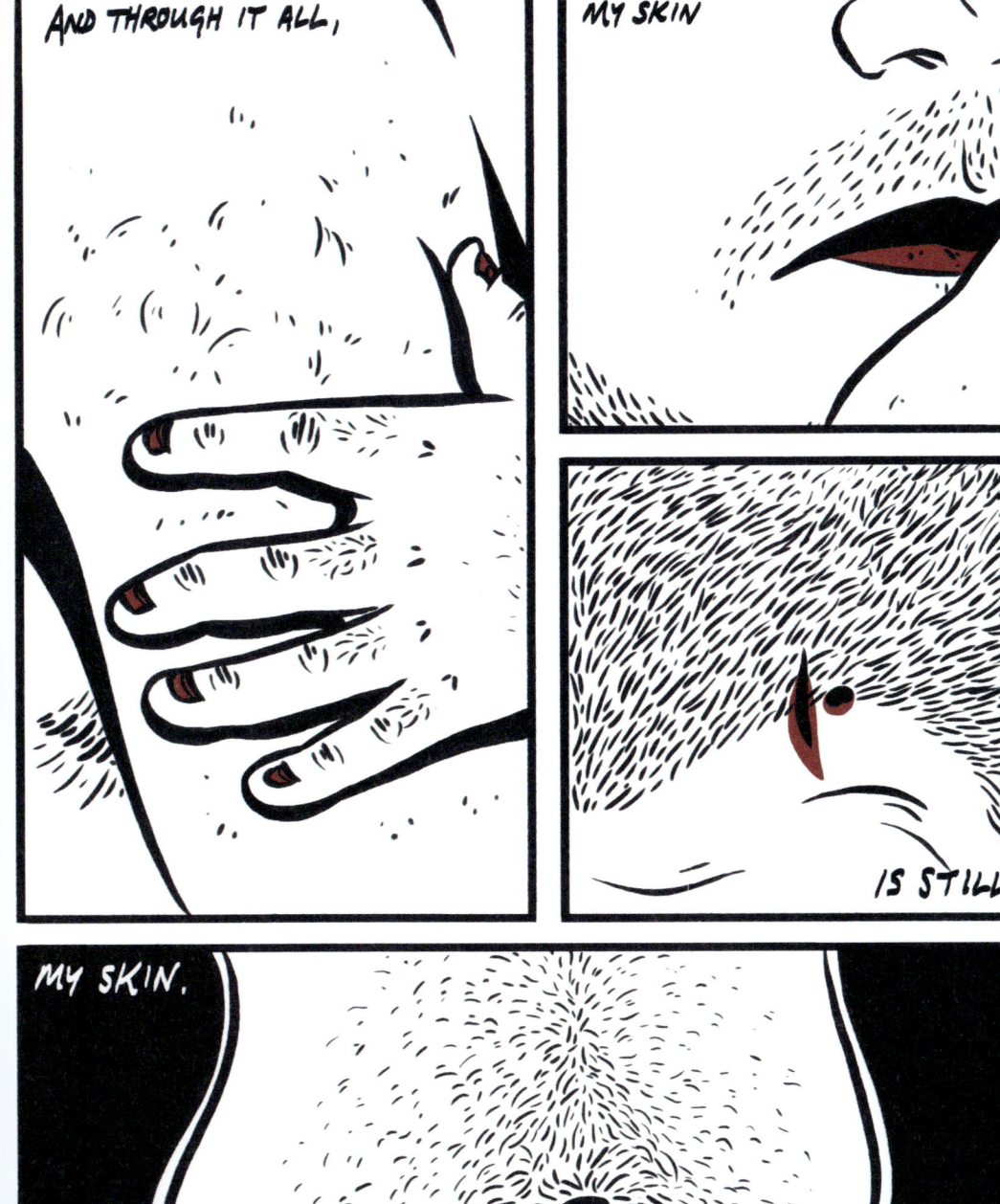

transbareall

Endnotes

Glossary of Terms

These words and definitions are mostly from day-to-day usage. They are largely Western Anglo-American terms, and other groups may use other language. We offer them not as a definitive guide to trans terminology, but to help make your reading experience easier. Language evolves, and different groups of people may use terms differently. You may therefore come across or have different definitions.

AFAB or AMAB
Assigned Female At Birth, or Assigned Male At Birth. This is used to describe what the midwife or doctor said at the moment of a person's birth, based on the outward appearance of the baby's genitals – either 'It's a girl' (AFAB) or 'It's a boy!' (AMAB)

Boi
Has many definitions, including:
    1) A term generally used to describe a submissive person in a kink relationship (especially if there is a Daddy/boi element to the power dynamic).
    2) Used within queer/trans communities to allow for a more masculine gender expression regarless of the gender assigned at birth.
    3) Used by people assigned female at birth (AFAB) who have a more masculine identity, and who may also use the term masculine of centre. This can also be connected to specific ethnic identities and experiences (often African American/Black).

Cis/Cisgender
Being comfortable with/identifying as the sex assigned at birth. From the Latin 'cis' which means 'on the same side of',

as opposed to 'trans' which means 'across, beyond, or on the other side'.

Cisnormative
The assumption that everyone's gender identity matches the sex they were assigned at birth. This assumption demands that we should act in line with, or be constrained by, ideas about gender that are socially expected at this time and in this culture.

Genderqueer
Identifying and/or presenting as being outside the gender binary of man/woman. May refer to someone who questions the whole idea of gender as a construct and who chooses not to be identified within that construct.

GIC
Gender Identity Clinic

Non-binary
A non-binary (sometimes shortened to 'enby') person identifies wholly with neither man nor woman. They may identify as somewhere in between, outside of, or a particular blend of both or neither of the 'binary' gender identities. This can also include gender fluid people, whose gender is not static.

People of colour/Person of colour/POC
POC is an inclusive term which means anyone who is not white. It includes people of mixed heritage, as well as lighter-skinned people who are not white.

Queer
This can mean many things and is very individual. For some

people who challenge binaries of gender and/or sexuality, it is a reclaimed term of abuse that is used with a sense of political defiance. For others it is a positive way of describing difference, or a label that is broad enough to contain a number of different sexual and gender minorities. Queer is still used as a slur against LGBT and gender non-conforming people, and some LGBT people do not like to use it for this reason.

T
An abbreviation for testosterone

Trans
We use the term trans as an inclusive term for anyone who self-defines in any way other than wholly with the sex they were assigned at birth. This could range from someone who transitions to a different gender either socially and/or medically, to someone who does not undergo transition but relates to a gender outside the one they were assigned at birth. It can be based on gender identity and/or gender expression, and includes non-binary, fluid, and related identities

We understand that not all people with these experiences may identify as trans, but instead may relate to having had a trans history, rather than a trans identity.

Trans feminine/Trans femme
Trans feminine describes trans people who identify with the more feminine part of the gender spectrum.

Trans masculine/Trans masc.
Trans masculine describes trans people who identify with the more masculine part of the gender spectrum.

transbareall

Biographies

TBA TEAM

Production Manager
Adam Lowe (he (mostly)/she (sometimes))
Adam is a writer, performer, publisher and creative producer. He teaches on the MA in Writing for Performance & Publication at the University of Leeds, founded LGBT writers collective Young Enigma and runs Dog Horn Publishing. Sometimes she performs as Beyonce Holes.

Alex Sanderson-Shortt (he/him)
Alex is a queer old bear. By day a therapist, sometimes writer, and general doer of things administrative. Having settled in the Cheshire countryside, he can still occasionally be found wandering the streets of Manchester reminiscing about marches and sit-ins and protests of old.

Amandeep Dhindsa (Amandeep/They)
Non Binary and Queer. Love all things central, so have settled in the midlands. Background in the legal field and now an Animator/photographer. As I live online and know no life before the internet, I am social media'ing' for TransBareAll. You can find me TWT, FB and YT by @a.n.dproductions and @arthousestudios

Dave Merchant (he/him)
Dave is not very good at writing stuff, especially about himself. He's much better at chatting, and can happily go on for hours on a number of topics, including Liverpool FC, 80s and 90s indie music, and why you should be in a union. Make him a peppermint tea, or buy him a pint of real ale, and you could be lucky (?) enough to experience this for yourself!

Emil (they/he)
Emil is a professional baker, aspiring filmmaker and a Co-Chair of TransBareAll. Currently living in Edinburgh, Scotland, Emil led the crowdfunding project to help bring this book to life.

Jack James-Fagg (they/he)
Jack is a small time doodler, time giver and general helper, but never has time to sit down and draw, so for this project they did just that. They have helped out with TBA for over five years, and they enjoy helping others and seeing people grow. During the day they are an office manager for a local charity. With the theory that there is a finite amount of organisation in the world for a person, Jack spends most of their organisation on work and TBA, which means their personal life is a little disorganised.

Jake Herrett (he/him or they/them)
Jake is a photographer, activist and cat lover. He is interested in creating safer spaces for marginalised people where they can be themselves, free from judgement. He has long been a central part of the TBA family in many different capacities and has been involved with the trans community in Manchester for over nine years.

Lee Gale (they/he)
Lee loves board games and being trans. They live most of their life in a trans bubble, which is perfect and just the way they think it should be. He is currently Co-Chair of TBA and it's his absolute passion - if you ask them about it, they can easily talk to you for days! His day job is as a Senior Trainer Consultant for Gendered Intelligence. Although he's an introvert, he loves to facilitate groups and stand up and talk about trans stuff in front of people.

Michelle Green (they)
Mish is an editor and creative facilitator who works with people at all levels of writing experience. As well as this gorgeous book, they recently co-edited *Indivisible*, Commonword's anthology of writing by authors with invisible disabilities. They have been part of the TBA team for four years now. Their formative gender role models were Boy George, Tank Girl, and the bronze cowboy statue on the hill near one of their childhood homes. Mish is an award-winning writer, performer and artist, interested in class, disability aesthetics, and maps, among other things: books and more at www.michellegreen.co.uk

ARTISTS

A Anon (he/they)
A Anon is a strange inverted goat-like creature who lives in the desert. He was cast out from his village bearing the sin and shame of the villagers in the form of rocks. When he broke them open, he found treasure inside. He lives a life of perfect contentment and is fabulously wealthy but nobody knows it except the goats. He would like to add a footnote to say that this is based on one person's experience with one doctor at one gender clinic. Many doctors are open to hearing non binary experience and provide excellent service and support to gender radicals in all our wonderful diversity. #notallgics

Alex Asher (they/them)
Hello, I am Alex, an 18 year old performance poet from Yorkshire. I write slam poetry about a variety of subjects, from education and politics, to mental health and of course,

being transgender. I've performed at different venues across West Yorkshire, alongside well-known, professional poets. I have also been interviewed on the radio and am featured in the Bradford Review.

You can find more of my work on YouTube: Alex Asher.

Allie Crewe (she/her)
Allie lives in Manchester and is a photographic artist. Having previously exhibited at the Getty Gallery and Lloyds of London, her portraits have met with critical acclaim. Described as 'Highly rated, sincere, poignant and classical...' by Magnum Photography, and as '...a terrific body of work filled with heart and empathy' by LensCulture, her work was shortlisted for the prestigious Portrait of Britain award in 2017 and she had a solo show in 2018. In 2019 her portrait of a trans woman, Grace, won the BJP Portrait of Britain.

www.allie-crewe.uk

Annabelle May Hampton (she)
Being trans dominated everything and despite several attempts to become more male than male, I failed miserably. My earliest memory of dressing was aged six. My mother did take me to the doctors, aged twelve. He told me to do plenty of cross country running! Finally, in September 2018 I had gender reassignment surgery at Charing Cross Hospital. I now identify as a transwoman. I am an artist, sometime poet, and storyteller, not necessarily in that order. I also work as a cleaner – it helps pay the rent, just!

Anonymous (he/him)
The author of this piece is male with a trans history and enjoys a quiet life living with his husband in a rural village. His passions include poetry, sketching and making jams and jellies. This is his second poem to be published, the first having been a competition winner several years prior to his transition. He has asked to remain anonymous so as to maintain some control over who knows of his trans experiences.

Apu (she/her)
Apu is a 37 year old queer non-binary & transfeminine punk, organic gardener/farmer and collage diy artist workin' and livin' on an organic seed breeding farm in northern germany. She's creatin' collage artwork for more than 18 years now (doin' a lot of co-ops with zines, bands, solidarity projects, collectives...) and is part of a small diy art collective named Theo Collective. In the last years Apu created collage artwork for different stunning projects, initiatives, zines, solidarity projects with topics like gender, anarcha-feminism, autonomous & cultural spaces, organic farming, diy ethics, mental health, selfcare, off grid living...

Twitter: @Apu_sometree & Instagram: @apu_sometree)

www.theobeam.wordpress.com/about/

Beebee Vanunu
Beebee has written for META magazine, Transparent, and has had her poetry published in the Manchester Review. She likes to work with mixed-media and has made *Luscious Drums*, a series of absurdist and satirical collages, sketches and poetry and *Buckmaster's Chariot* which is an anti-narrative incomprehensible

jumble of what she thinks are good-sounding words. She was formerly the loud drummer in Tuck & the Binders, performs solo musical shows as Lady Diabolical and is working on her first shareable recorded music. She is currently very enthusiastic about learning how to play darbuka and Kendrick Lamar. She is of mixed Moroccan and English heritage, from a working-class background and was born in Blackpool. She has only recently come out of creative hiding after a long struggle with borderline disorder and addiction issues, and is proud of her scars.

Ben Hattingh (he/they)
Ben has been writing prose and poetry since their teen years and used their passion for writing to complete a Creative Writing BA (hons) at Sheffield Hallam. 'Bluebells' was developed from a final year poetry portfolio, Kindling. In more recent years, Ben has focused on screenwriting and successfully competed for a place in the National Youth Film Academy.

You can find Ben on LinkedIn, and additionally on Instagram: @ben.zamo

Benjen (they/them)
Benjen is a queer non-binary bear who has found home in West Yorkshire. You'll most likely find them six hours deep into a Buffy marathon or scuttling between patches of shade in a woodland. When they're not lighting fires or whittling spoons, they are working towards setting up a community centre in a neglected urban woodland using recycled and reused materials, offering space for people to explore things like self sustenance and food sovereignty.

Find out more by following @redbearoutdoors.cic on facebook.

Beth Charley

Beth is a 30-something mixed race disabled femme. She is starting a new chapter in her life after spending two years trying to achieve a Masters in Autism Studies. She hopes that the past decade of exploring life will help cultivate a more creative and sustainable future, but currently is really struggling with her mental health. She is grateful for this opportunity as it is her first published accomplishment since winning a poetry competition in primary school, writing about raindrops.

BJ Christie (he/him)

It has been said that within every person's life there are the makings of a book. Some are merely pamphlets, some are torrid bodice-rippers or could even be thrillers.

Others are soaring, achingly powerful epics that leave the reader in an emotionally depleted heap, desperate to reread and wondering how it could possibly be all true. When Ben gets around to writing his, it will be the latter. Until he hits the bestseller lists, you can find him currently enjoying a very happy and busy life as husband, mother, grandpa, carpenter and policeman.

Caleb M (they/them)

Caleb is a 28 year old non-binary writer, who currently resides in Scotland. Their main preference of work is poetry, but they also dabble in short stories and at times the epistolary form. Caleb has experienced emotionally challenging events, from family bereavement to recovering from kidney cancer. They often joke that the scar from surgery on the kidney makes it look like they have been in a fight with a shark, and won!

Outside of writing, Caleb spends far too much time gaming, delving down the weird side of youtube and mindless internet browsing.

Chris
Chris, now in their late thirties, has had connections to trans people since their teens. Peer connections, in parallel with the growing online communities, were formative for Chris's self-understanding as non-binary, even when binary identities and linear medical transitions predominated. They attended the first TBA retreat. In the last few years, Chris has also come to understand themself as autistic.

Connor Rose (he/him)
Connor is a single dad and trans guy who enjoys making art and baking cakes in Scotland. When he was younger, teachers at school told him he was no good at art, and now that he's older he has learnt to ignore that kind of opinion and do what makes him happy.

www.instagram.com/queer_saints/

www.facebook.com/QueerSaints/

Crake Dakini
Crake is; a brief elaboration of a tube, Buddhist and autistic polymath. Currently residing in 'The land of no more fucks to give' with several pets, and a surprising number of axes. Where they await the zombie apocalypse. They spend their time mastering spheres of expertise (that they don't already have degrees in), and running round the countryside after their three legged dog, who likes to lollop off and hide under

holly thickets. They hope to live long enough to witness the apocalypse, having once almost died after being bitten by a pet rat.

Daniel Morrison (he/they)
Daniel is a therapist, writer and parent living in North Wales. He's studying Gender, Sexuality and Culture MA at Manchester University. He also facilitates workshops for the LGBTQ+ community around consent, energy and conscious connection. He's currently involved in organising Queer Spirit festival which means he's googled yurt hire so much the internet thinks he's getting married. He's not.

Danielle Hopkins
Danielle has a wide and varied background in life. Having transitioned whilst homeless, she makes it a priority to help others so that they do not have to go through the same as she has. Passionate and driven, she has appeared in film, in print and online as a retro games authority, and has had spells on the stage, mainly as an extra. She currently wonders where the next adventure in life will take her after helping gender, homelessness, mental health and substance misuse charities for the last five years or so.

Devon Bacso (she/they)
Devon is an East Coast transplant currently living in Tucson, Arizona. They work as a school psychologist with aspirations of being a doula. Their hobbies include making bad pottery, watching any Dateline episode hosted by Keith Morrison, and cuddling with their adorable two cats.

Eilatan Hunter (he/him)

Eilatan lives and works in London. This is my first piece of creative writing since I did A level English. This piece was fun to write and I might take it up creative writing again in the future. Outside of work as a histologist I spend time in nature, walking or camping with friends. Aside from that I love to spend my time researching how to optimize my wellbeing and mind.

Frank Duffy (they/them)

Frank Duffy is a graphic designer, illustrator and printmaker who has an MA with distinction from Falmouth. They grew up in a very normal suburb of Cardiff and thus are delighted to now be living in a static caravan on a beautiful 20 acre smallholding in rural Carmarthenshire with fellow queers, rare butterflies, waterfalls and plastic flamingos. Their work explores the spaces between the cracks – gender, magic, power and death.

They are MxFrankDuffy on twitter and instagram, and they have a Patreon where they share their writing and images and send out limited edition prints as rewards – www.patreon.com/acuriousqueer

Franki Ayres

Franki is an Artist living and working in London.

If you want to find out more, or view other works, please do contact – franki.a.ayres@gmail.com.

Harry Robin Hunkin (they/them)
Harry is a proud redhead who was born and raised in Nottingham. They finished their degree in English and Creative Writing at the University of Nottingham with a poetry dissertation which focused around exploration of their trans and non-binary identity. When not writing, Harry is a tattoo enthusiast and cat person who copes with the hardships of life by smooshing their face into the soft tummy of one of their three pet Voids (otherwise known as Hubble, Pluto, and Nova, their black cats).

Hidden Ink Child (they/them)
Hidden Ink Child is a self taught artist, poet, author, photographer and zine maker. They create and have featured in multiple zines & publications, and they have exhibited film, installation and printed work at exhibitions relation to mental health since 2017. They spend their spare time in public libraries or swimming in the sea.

Instagram @hiddeninkchild

Jacob S (he/him or they/them)
Jacob is a trans masc person with a beard, a belly and a baby that he gave birth to. He's proud of all that he is and all that he's achieved and he tells anyone who'll listen that TBA has been life changing for him.

Jochem
Jochem is an experienced Dutch trans activist. He has done much for transmen in particular, like starting Transman.nl and founding Transman Foundation. Jochem met Lee for the first time in 2008, at the 2nd Transgender Europe Council in Berlin. And again at following TGEU Councils. In 2011 Jochem

attended his first TBA. That inspired him to start the Dutch Trans & Bare Weekends in 2015. In mundane life, Jochem was a self employed coach and energy worker, but had to stop due to chronic illness. Now he is a queer & disability activist.

You can read his blog at jochemverdonk.nl.

Jonathan Fernandez (he/him)
Jonathan has been involved in Jewish learning since he converted to Judaism two years ago. He has studied the Talmud (Jewish oral law and commentary) at Svara, an LGBTQ+ Talmud programme in the US, the Open Talmud Project and Marom Talmud shiur, and he is part of the organising team for the Open Talmud Project 2019. He is passionate about finding ways to include and celebrate diverse experiences in Torah (Jewish teaching, culture, holy text, practise) and Jewish life. He lives in North London with his partner and cat.

Joni Grace Indolent (she/her)
Joni is an artist from Manchester. Best known for her monochromatic, punk / DIY aesthetic she combines photography, inks, paints and digital manipulation to create striking and thought provoking imagery. Her work can be found in the form of posters, clothing and accessories for her own brand, Indolent Clothing, as well as for a variety of independent musicians. A prolific graffiti artist and live art competition winner, she specialises in philosophical, cultural and political statement pieces where she draws influence from classic movie posters, late 19th / early 20th century propaganda, medieval woodcut prints, and documentary photography.

@WeAreIndolent

Kira Nelson (she/her)

Kira has been writing since she was eight years old when she began work on her very own sequel to her favourite book series, *Harry Potter*. After she discovered the meaning of the word plagiarism, she started writing stories of her own. She is currently working on a dystopian adventure novel, which she hopes to then convert into a motion picture or even a video game. 'The Straw Man' is her first publication.

Leo Alexander

Leo has been writing poetry and stories (of varying quality) since childhood. Now living mostly as a student in London, he usually incorporates irony, dark humour and musings on modern life in his writing. In between writing papers and debating, he keeps a poetry blog.

www.parliamentofowlsblog.wordpress.com

Léo Taylor

Léo was born in Lincolnshire. They have worked in scientific research and currently teach science in secondary education. They also facilitate workshops around mental health at the LGBT Foundation in Manchester. While their journey so far has at times been uncertain, their ultimate aim is to make use of their collected experience and passions in a counselling career. Léo's poetic writing has been a lifelong hobby and creative outlet for their love of languages.

Leslie Tate (Leslie)

Appearing in the Danish Genderhouse and the rock/words festival Louder Than Words, Leslie Tate collaborates with artists, musicians and filmmakers. Leslie studied Creative

Writing with the University of East Anglia and has been shortlisted for the Bridport, Geoff Stevens and Wivenhoe Prizes. He/she/Leslie is the author of the trilogy of novels *Purple*, *Blue* and *Violet*, about modern love, as well as a non-binary memoir *Heaven's Rage*, now an indie film showing at thirty two international film festivals. Leslie interviews people weekly about their creativity at

www.leslietate.com

Little Frank (they)
Physics nerd, yogi, dog parent, worm farmer. Political Queer, political Crip, autistic, mentally ill. Loves gardening, vegan food, and listening to stories. Non binary. Frank is very tired of ignorant shits telling them what they can and can't do with their own body.

Logan Turner (he/they)
Lives in Scotland with his partner Emil and their two cats Bo and Kobi. Logan has always liked to use creative outlets such as drawing and painting. This is his first publication.

Louis Bailey (he/him)
Louis lives in, and is obsessed with, the Dark Peak. An academic by day and a fell runner by night, he is currently working on his first piece of creative non-fiction, *The Night Run*, which celebrates rural queerness, mythology and the art of 'failure'. He is the co-founder of ArtMob – a visual arts platform for trans and non-binary artists in the UK – and was the co-curator of *Continuum: Framing Trans Lives in 21st Century Britain* at the People's History Museum, Manchester. His work has been published in a range of peer-reviewed journals, academic texts

and poetry anthologies.

www.artmob.co.uk

Ludo Tolu (they/them)
Ludo is Mediterranean but has called the UK their home for the past five years. They currently live and study in Cambridge, with their partner and house plants. This is their first short story.

Ludovic Foster (he/him/his)
Ludovic is an independent academic, community worker, fine artist, curator, and avid swimmer. He holds a PhD in Gender Studies from the University of Sussex for his thesis *Narratives of Tomboy Identity in Fiction and Film: Exploring a Hidden History*.

A Bob Dylan enthusiast, Ludovic has a chapter 'Beyond the Horizon: Observing the Queerness within Bob Dylan's Gesture' in an upcoming publication by the University Press of Southern Denmark. He has also been involved with LGBTQi and disability projects, and facilitated addiction recovery awareness workshops. Originally from South Wales, Ludovic presently resides in East Sussex UK.

www.instagram.com/ludoboi/

Mx Lupin
Hi I'm Mx Lupin. I'm nonbinary and I currently study philosophy and creative writing at university. I am very much obsessed with absorbing as much knowledge as I can about the universe. I also do spoken word performances and draw here and there. My hope is to continuously write things that cause

a paradigm shift, so that I can be a part of positive progression in the world; helping break away all the different ways living beings are segregated by hierarchies and social constructions and instead bring back wildness to all nature.

Max Alexander (he/him)
Max is a visual artist and quiet poet based in Edinburgh, Scotland. He's a queer autistic nature boy who heavily-identifies with Snufkin from the Moomin-verse. He is currently working on finding ways to share his art with others because when he does, he feels pretty-nice about it.

Melody Sproates (they/them)
Melody is a writer and performer based in Newcastle. They make challenging and sometimes daft work to help represent the underrepresented, break binaries and to just have a bit of a dance to some bops. They have just completed their debut solo show *gender not included*, a lip sync performance about gender identity and self acceptance, which will be touring Spring 2020.

Instagram: @melodygrooovysproates

Facebook: @melodysproatesperformer

Ms. Mocha Slessor-Parks (MichaelShe)
Ms Mocha is a poet and academic resident in Makurdi, Nigeria. She is passionate about psycho-social support structures for trans women. Also, she mentors trans women and is actively involved in accessible healthcare for trans women in heteronormative communities. She envisages equitable societies where trans women will thrive despite dominant narratives (especially in Nigeria) fueled by cultural and religious influences. Mocha

works with RURCHEDI (Twitter: @MakurdiRurchedi) and other partners researching into the situation of sexual minorities in Nigeria and advocacy against Conversion Therapies.

Nathan Gale
Nathan is a non-binary, queer, crip who uses poetry, performance and visual art as part of their activism to challenge systems of oppression. Their poetry and visual art have been featured at exhibitions at the Gallery of Modern Art in Glasgow, the MAC in Birmingham and Schwules Museum in Berlin. Nathan has been privileged to perform their poetry around Europe, highlights include DaDafest, Cachin Cachan Cachunga Queer and Trans Cabaret, the Edinburgh Fringe, and Wigstockel Berlin.

Neal Bowman (he)
Neal is a medical doctor and has worked on four continents providing anaesthetic services to paediatric and adult patients including 'flying doctors' in Australia, 'operation smile' – a cleft palate charity in Africa and working as a consultant and professor in anaesthesia in the UK NHS and USA. His writings include clinical research published in peer reviewed medical journals and for lighter relief – 'slash' fanfiction including genres such as sci-fi (*Star Trek* and *Doctor Who*) and US procedural shows such as *White Collar* and *Kyle XY*.

His stories can be found under the username 'fishiexy' at fanfiction.net.

Oliver Bonnell (he/him)
Oliver is an artist living in Sheffield working with 3D modelling,

animation, and design software. He creates scenes depicting the side effects on the self and nature, arising from issues such as prevailing homogeneity, kyriarchy, and capitalism. His use of computer software allows him to create complex worlds, as detailed as a photograph, but with the freedom to depict an entirely surreal reality. He currently draws inspiration from his experience of years in economic uncertainty and precarious accommodation contrasted with the positive influence of community, love, friendship and queer family.

Ollie Scharaschkin (they/them)
Ollie is a queer human - being, dreaming and healing.

Rahil Cyril Virik (they/them)
Rahil is a 25-year-old British Asian Non-Binary person. Born in Leicester, they now live in South London and work as a Counsellor, Youth Worker and Trainer. They are passionate about developing their work for and within the LGBT and POC communities. Having recently returned to writing as a creative outlet, they wish to explore themes of diversity, resilience, warmth and healing.

You can find them on Instagram @rahilcyrilvirik.

Rami Yasir
Rami is a poet, illustrator, workshop facilitator and youth worker of Sudani and Jordanian-Palestinian descent. They explore the themes of gender, race, home and love in their work on the page and do their best to help others express themselves creatively and productively in their workshops. They enjoy dogs, sleeping, long walks on the beach, and making art when they get a chance to. They're very good. You should book them.

Instagram: @ramiyasir

Twitter: @YasirRami

Facebook: @ramimilkyasir

Email: ramimilkyasir@gmail.com

Remi Butler (she/her)
Remi is a programmer and hobbyist writer and you can find more of her gubbins on twitter @ctrlaltcookie

Roadmap Zach (he/him)
Hey, hello, hi! Roadmap Zach is a sunshine chaser, lover of music, and dancing badly. He enjoys bringing people together, and aspires to open a LGBTQ+ café and hub in his hometown. When he finally sits down to focus, he considers himself an avid snapshot taker/filmmaker and wannabe writer/spoken word poet.

You can find him on YouTube: RoadmapZach

Robin Hob (they/them or he/his)
Robin has more ideas than time and is on a constant quest to find balance and compromise in their life. They have worked incredibly hard, and are very grateful that they have a job in their chosen career of psychology; a career that is a source of great joy, and many frustrations. Robin is keen to create spaces where community and inclusion are central, whether that be festivals, workshops, conferences or writings. They enjoy quiet time, woods and canals, reading, learning, questioning and moving their body in a multitude of ways.

Robin Prior (he/him)
Robin has been writing ever since he could hold a pen, discovering a deep love for poetry at a young age. Robin would spend his time at school scribbling down short poems and passing them to his friends. After he balled one up and threw it across the table for his best friend to read he was dismissed from the class and sent to sit in with the older children as punishment. However, when the teacher finally came to collect him he didn't want to leave because they were having a great time reading *Oliver Twist*, and he didn't want to return to learning about triangles. Confused, his teacher decided it was best to leave him there for the rest of the day.

Sahaf Hardouf
I'm a queer trans Jew who's passionate about promoting LGBTQIA+ inclusion in faith spaces. I work for a trans charity and I'm also involved in Jewish and interfaith community work in the UK, Israel and Palestine.

Sam Hill
Sam is an End of Life Doula supporting others to live and die authentically. Through a personal journey of becoming congruent they have used creativity to consider their own identity, finding their transgender self within this. A freelance writer who enjoys photography and delving into the abstract, Sam loves experimenting with words across all genres. Inspired by the natural world, spirituality, sexuality and gender they use poetry, personal essays and stream of consciousness to explore these topics. Sam lives in Brighton with their partner and two cats, enjoys being by the sea, practicing mindfulness and eating chips.

Website: www.identitythroughcreativity.com
Instagram: @identitythroughcreativity

Sebastian Buser (he/they)
Sebastian is an ardent walker; they love to roam through cities, up mountains and organises walks for queers in the countryside. He is an artist and an architectural researcher who aims to shine a light on queer DIY spaces, finding these architectural delights to be the most inspiring and often overlooked in the 'big' world of architectural history and theory. He completed his MA in Architectural History at the Bartlett School of Architecture (UCL) last year and will be commencing his PhD in September. Sebastian has taken part in several art exhibitions and performances but this is their first written publication.

Serkan Kasapoğlu
Serkan is passionate about provoking the patriarchal-oppressive society they live in by their appearance and attitude. Serkan is originally from Bulgaria but lives in Turkey. They are studying Western Languages and Literature at Boğaziçi University. As an advocate, Serkan makes LGBTQIA+ people more visible in their universities and advocates for sex workers' rights. They is also a drag queen.

You can follow her on instagram: @svety.beauty

Sez Thomasin (they/them)
Sez is an autistic, genderqueer social justice worrier, youth worker and poet. They marvel at the grammatical knots many cis people tie themselves in trying to manage their they/them pronouns, but them does appreciates the effort. Sez lives in Sheffield and enjoys cooking strange meats.

Simon Croft (he/him)
Simon is a trans-man living and working in London. He transitioned 21 years ago, and began making visual art at roughly the same time, completing a Fine Art degree in 2006. He uses a variety of materials and techniques including small object making, paper cutting, installation, collage and video, making work that stems from his trans experience, but often engages around gender more broadly. His work has been shown in London, Amsterdam, Berlin and San Francisco. In his day job, Simon works for Gendered Intelligence, encouraging the world to become more intelligent when it comes to gender!

www.simon-croft.co.uk

Simon Williamson (he/him)
Simon is an illustrator and animator based in Sheffield. His first published comic was included in the *We're Still Here* anthology, released by Stacked Deck Press in 2018. He is passionate about creating more LGBT representation in film and graphic arts, and empowering LGBT creators to tell stories that speak to them. When Simon's not drawing, he can be found tending to his very pampered guinea pigs.

You can find his work at instagram.com/simonisnotanartist.

Rob Clucas (he)
Rob is a queer academic who lives in the North of England. He has been a voracious reader and writer since he was five. He loves his job but probably ought to spend less time working. His hobbies include cycling and creating things with wool; the love of his life so far is his recently deceased cat.

Tom of Tottenham

Tom of Tottenham is a Black british queer leather Daddy. Tom is an activist, filmmaker, producer and performer. Tom enjoys and makes porn. Tom is on FetLife, come say hello: Tom_Kink

Ynda Jas (they)

Ynda is a queer non-binary transfemme activist, socialist, creative, lapsed academic and developing coder. They're the founder of Non-binary London and York LGBTQ+ History, and DJ coordinator at the iconic weekly queer cabaret event Bar Wotever (at the Royal Vauxhall Tavern). They're also a poet, music producer, tennis enthusiast and gamer.

Twitter/Instagram: @yndajas

transbareall

Acknowledgements

Firstly, we would like to give a special thanks to Michelle Green. Your enthusiasm, skill and energy have pushed this book to its absolute potential.

You held people's work with such tenderness, respect and compassion, understanding the vulnerable nature people put themselves in by offering their creative works and personal stories. It was a privilege to see you in action and to see the work develop and flourish under your skilled guidance.

Without you this book would never have happened and we appreciate all you have done to bring the book to life.

We love you ♥

Frank Duffy

A project like this takes a lot of time and effort from many people in many ways – and a bit of money too! We'd like to say a massive thank you to everyone who has been involved, in whatever way they could. This book would not exist without you.

We see you, we love you and we celebrate with you!

The TBA management team:
* Michelle Green
* Lee Gale
* Dave Merchant
* Emil Green
* Jake Herrett
* Jack James-Fagg
* Amandeep Kaur
* Alex Sanderson-Shortt

The book production and design team:
* Adam Lowe - Project Management
* Frank Duffy - Design
* Ryan Combs - Transcription
* Greg Thorpe - consultation in the early days!

Contributors:
A huge thanks to all the people who submitted their work to us: for their time, skills, patience, and willingness to share and be vulnerable. The editorial process was a close one that focused heavily on artist development, and without exception all of our contributors engaged with that process with heart and openness. Thank you. This is yours.

Financial support:

This project was made possible by the generous support of our funders, without whom you would not hold this book in your hands. Our huge thanks and appreciation to Arts Council England, and the LGBT+ Consortium.

Charity Number:
1105502

Personal donations through our crowdfunder:
Huge thanks to all of our crowdfunder supporters, with special thanks to:

Blue Swain
Cameron Steward
Carolyn & Dennis Bailey
DK Green
Emma Cuthbertson
Estelle Bridgewater
Jed Jerwood
Jill Gale
Keir Gale
Liam Mercer
Robert Softley Gale
Simon Croft

Practical support:
LGBT Foundation

Commonword

All those who retweeted, reblogged and reposted and spread the word about our project, especially Rainbow Noir – thank you for the love!

Previous TBA Team Members:
We would like to thank all our previous team members for their amazing work over the past 10 years. You have all brought something special to TBA and are held in our hearts:
Jay
Ellis
Nathan
Rob
Maeve
Elliott

How to support us

TBA is a grassroots organisation run entirely by volunteers. We receive no government funding (national or local), nor any regular grants from larger organisations. We are funded almost entirely on an event-to-event basis, where the attendance fees from one event help to pay for the next.

Our aim is to provide a series of retreats and parties at which trans people and cis allies can meet, and offer and recieve support in a safer space.

In order to carry on doing this, we need support.

Donate to TBA
All of the money we make is used directly to put on retreats and parties. We don't pay any of the team or have many admin overheads. You can be sure that your donation is helping to keep the events accessible by keeping costs low, and enabling us to offer financial assistance (like travel grants) for those who might otherwise not be able to come.

You can donate by
Bank Account:
Trans Bare All
Sort code: 30-98-97
Account No: 52428368
Setting up a standing order of a few pounds a month.

Send us money via Paypal:
transbareall@gmail.com

Signing up to EasyFundraising; once you sign up, when you shop online at affiliated businesses they donate a small portion to us, at no cost to you! https://www.easyfundraising.org.uk/causes/transbareall/

While money is great, there are many other ways you can get involved to help us carry on this important work.

You can also support us by:

Attending a retreat or party! Having a good turn out makes the event more successful, and helps build a sense of community and connection that remains after the event has finished.

Talking about us. Sharing your experiences and talking to your family, friends and colleagues is a great way of building awareness of issues affecting us, and building a powerful force for positive change.

Social media. Sharing your thoughts on social media helps spread the word, and builds a sense of community.

Running a workshop. We always ask our attendees to propose, plan and run the workshops at the parties to ensure that it is a truly grassroots event. Let us know if you have any ideas for future workshops, skill shares, discussions or activities you'd like to offer! We are experienced facilitators and can help with this, so you don't have to do it alone.

Being an ally. Be an ally by supporting trans groups, educating yourself on the issues, using your voice to allow trans people's voices to be heard, and challenging transphobia when you encounter it.